D1116677

By the same Author

ONOMASTICON OF PALESTINE

A NEW METHOD
IN POST-BIBLICAL TOPOGRAPHY

with a preface by
PROFESSOR CHARLES C. TORREY

NEW YORK
1937

THE AMERICAN ACADEMY FOR JEWISH RESEARCH
3080 Broadway, N. Y. C.

PRICE ONE DOLLAR

JEWISH SYMBOLS ON ANCIENT JEWISH COINS

PAUL ROMANOFF

(1899–1943)

JEWISH SYMBOLS ON ANCIENT JEWISH COINS

PAUL ROMANOFF, Ph.D.

Museum
Jewish Theological Seminary of America

With an Introduction by

ABRAHAM A. NEUMAN

President, The Dropsie College

29808

PHILADELPHIA

THE DROPSIE COLLEGE FOR HEBREW AND COGNATE LEARNING

1944

Copyright, 1944, by
Louis S. Werner

PRINTED IN THE UNITED STATES OF AMERICA
PRESS OF THE JEWISH PUBLICATION SOCIETY
PHILADELPHIA, PENNA.

CONTENTS

CJ1375
.R63

INTRODUCTION

by

ABRAHAM A. NEUMAN

IT IS my sad privilege to write an Introduction to this important study by an alumnus of the Dropsie College, Doctor Paul Romanoff, whose untimely death was a grievous loss to scholarship and a source of bereavement to those who were bound to him in life by bonds of friendship and ties of love.

Numismatics as an auxiliary science to history is noted for its fascination rather than for the illumination of the facts of history. When a nation has reached the stage of issuing coins, it has generally emerged from historic obscurity and the coins rarely add to the basic facts already known from other less cryptic and more voluble sources of information.

Among other classic nations, the coins bear images of emperors, kings and military leaders, which are, as a rule, faithful contemporary portraits. Their value is chiefly extra-historical. They depict the character of the men who were the embodiment of their nation's history. They often serve as a valuable commentary on the character of the nation itself. These coins are important, too, as works of art. They are frequently the clearest expressions of the creative art of the nation. Furthermore, the royal coins, which bear an imperial portrait, usually carry on the reverse side a subject, sacred or mythological in character. These subjects reflect in crystallized form the religious rites and beliefs of the nation. Among a people like the Greeks, whose ritual and religious ceremonials were not preserved in literary codifications, the symbolic representations depicted on the coins are most illuminating. They depict in pictorial form the standardized customs and rites connected with the worship of the various local and national deities.

Jewish coins, by contrast, lack the characteristics which give importance to other coins of the same period. They bear no human image and hence have no value from the standpoint of portraiture. As for the religious symbols, at best they are only corroborative of the information which is known with far greater authenticity and accuracy from the abundant Hebrew religious literature. It is not surprising, therefore, that Jewish numismatics has, on the whole, not been cultivated with the same zeal which has been shown to other aspects of Jewish history.

On the other hand, it must be recognized that numismatics has special pertinence for a period of three hundred years of the most formative period of Jewish history, from the revolt of the Maccabees to the catastrophe of Bar Kokba. Doctor Sukenik, through the proper reading of the coins of the earlier Persian period, illustrated the fact that Palestine was an autonomous province before the advent of Alexander the Great. The title, priest instead of king, attached to the name of the head of the state struck on a coin, may arbitrate a conflict between Strabo and Josephus as to the status of Judas Aristobulus. By the presence or absence of foreign artistic models on the Jewish coins, one may trace the course of Jewish emancipation from Hellenism or subservience to foreign domination. The propaganda of Bar Kokba, to use Doctor Romanoff's term, is revealed in the coins, struck by the rebels, in their appeal to the undying hope of the people for the restoration of the Temple and the return of God's presence and grace among them. Above all, Jewish numismatics has a romantic appeal peculiar to our own time. Its subject, coins and coinage, is the symbol of national sovereignty. Only a free, autonomous nation had the right to strike coins. With the defeat of Bar Kokba, Jewish coinage ceased and Jewish numismatics became an antiquarian science. The revival of the hope of the restoration of Jewish sovereignty in Palestine has awakened a new vital interest in numismatics among Jewish scholars in Palestine, as symbolized in the researches of Sukenik, Reifenberg and Romanoff, whose interest in the subject dates back to the period of his life in Palestine.

The present work, *Jewish Symbols on Ancient Jewish Coins*, is an original and unique contribution to Jewish numismatics. The original motif of this work lies principally in the treatment of the symbols as a homogeneous group with a central theme. The author was not content to identify individual coins and to interpret their symbols. He sought and found a unifying principle amidst the varied types, or symbols, on the Jewish coins. This method not only aided him greatly in solving a number of obscure subjects; it afforded him an historic perspective by means of which he was able to delineate historic trends, folk psychology, national feelings and reactions during the political upheavals that characterized the period associated with Jewish numismatics.

Doctor Romanoff grouped the types around several themes: agriculture, the Temple building, astronomical subjects, and various significant utensils connected with the Temple service in which musical instruments were also utilized. While some of the types, such as the palm, the pomegranate, the lily and the lyre are to be found on non-Jewish coins as well, these symbols had a specific meaning in the national and religious consciousness of the Jews. Doctor Romanoff rightly interprets these themes through the eyes and hearts of the Jewish people contemporary with the coins. Through these symbols he sees the simple faith of the people, their trust in God and the blessings of nature, divinely controlled. No human deification, no animal sacrifices or pouring of blood upon the altar is to be found among the emblems. In contrast, Romanoff points to the contemporary non-Jewish symbols on the coins of the pagan cities and provinces of Palestine. They bear the imprint of deities, warriors and rulers; records of wars and conquests; pictorial representations of soldiers trampling upon the bodies of their fallen enemies, and the ploughing under of conquered cities.

Doctor Romanoff follows the same method with equal psychological penetration in the historical grouping of the symbols in the more usual chronological sequence: the Maccabean period and the First and the Second Revolt. In every period, the symbols reflect the dominant religious mood of the nation. The cycle of the three festivals, Passover, Pentecost and Tabernacles, supply the key motif of the symbolism when the Temple was still in existence. After the destruction of the Temple, the pictorial representation of the Sanctuary on the coins struck during the Second Revolt became the visible manifestation of the national yearning of the return of the divine presence in a free and independent Judean state.

By this treatment, Doctor Romanoff drew forth from the metallic objects the human voice of religious hope and national aspiration. He brought to bear upon this work not alone the expert knowledge and technique of the numismatist. He drew upon the rich resources of a wide range of rabbinical literature to illumine the symbols. In addition, he brought to his subject a knowledge and love of the land, its flowers, trees and vegetation, as well as an intuitive insight into the romantic yearnings and aspirations of his people which is nurtured in the atmosphere of Palestine.

This blend of the man, the scholar and the technician, Romanoff had previously exhibited in his work on Palestine topography, *The Onomasticon of Palestine: A New Method in Post-Biblical Topography.* Whereas other scholars in this field were chiefly concerned with the mere identification of place names, Romanoff pleaded for a new method and perspective, one which involved a critical examination of the ancient texts and which brought to the foreground the human personalities connected with those places, their biographic data, the lore and legends which were associated with the places.

In both fields, topography and numismatics, Doctor Romanoff made fresh contributions by proposing a new method of approach. In both cases, the method grew out of an intimate knowledge of the land, the people and its classic literature, a knowledge which was applied with the deftness of an artist and a trained technician.

Romanoff's interest in the symbolism of coins was only part of a wider appreciation and love of aesthetics in general. This is illustrated in a series of brief monographs: *The Hand as a Symbol in Art* as illustrated in *The Hand of God* (from the Bible to Michelangelo);[1] *The Symbolism and the Aesthetics of the Ancient Jewish Costume*;[2] *A Family of Illuminators in the Time of the Second Temple.*[3] These are but a small number of his miniature studies, which reveal the many-sided facets of an artistic soul.[4] He was the ideal

[1] *Bodn*, A Quarterly Review, ed. by N. B. Minkoff, Vol. I, pp. 61–72, (1934).

[2] Ibid. I, pp. 73–82.

[3] *JQR.*, XXVI (1935), pp. 29–35.

[4] For other examples, see I. Rivkind's fine appreciation, *Zukunft*, XLIX, pp. 115–19.

Curator of the Museum of Jewish Ceremonial Objects of the Jewish Theological Seminary, a position which he held from the establishment of the Museum in 1932 until his death on December 12, 1943.

Romanoff was unusually well equipped for those romantic excursions into the realm of Jewish art and scholarship. He was born in Vilna, April 19, 1898, a center of Jewish piety and learning, famed as the "Jerusalem of Lithuania." His father was an architect by profession, a saint in life, and his mental habitat was in the realm of the Talmud. From his father, young Romanoff drew the inspiration which determined his studies and the course of his life. He was equally at home in the Yeshibah as in the Gymnasium of Vilna, from which he graduated in 1915. He was a student during the German military occupation and later an officer in the Lithuanian Army. Subsequently, he continued his studies in Berlin and in Paris. In Palestine, which he entered in 1920, he applied his knowledge technically as architect of the Palestine Jewish Archaeological Society during the first campaign of the Excavations of the Third Wall in Jerusalem, and also served the Government of Palestine in similar capacity in the architectural and topographical work of the Department of Public Works. Simultaneously he continued his talmudic and rabbinical studies and entered the Hebrew University in 1925, where an impetus was given to his topographical interests by the late Professor Samuel Klein, which was further strengthened by Professor Max L. Margolis at the Dropsie College, where Romanoff entered in 1927 and received his Doctorate in 1930.

A graduate Fellowship at Yale University and the personal encouragement of Professor Charles C. Torrey helped to bring forth his introductory work on topography, *Onomasticon of Palestine: A New Method in Post-Biblical*

Topography. The impetus to the present work, *Jewish Symbols on Ancient Jewish Coins*, was due to two devoteés of numismatics: the late Edward T. Newell, President of the American Numismatic Society, and Louis S. Werner, Fellow of that Society. Through the good offices of Mr. Werner, Mr. Newell invited Doctor Romanoff to deliver a lecture on Jewish coins out of which grew the present work. In these researches, Doctor Romanoff was encouraged by the intense interest which these friends showed in the progress of the work, and he was aided considerably by the use of their magnificent collections, casts, slides, readings and other valuable information at their disposal. In addition to many other evidences of devotion and friendship, Louis S. Werner, Fellow of the American Numismatic Society, prepared the coin plates and the coin plate-index in this volume.

This work appeared initially in serial form in the *Jewish Quarterly Review* (XXXIII–XXXIV). Its welcome appearance in book form is due to the initiative and zeal of his devoted wife, Bertha Romanoff.

Abraham A. Neuman

Dropsie College, June 26, 1944.

JEWISH SYMBOLS ON ANCIENT JEWISH COINS

By Paul Romanoff

Museum of the Jewish Theological Seminary of America

Chapter I

Symbols, known as types in numismatic terminology,[1] on Jewish coins are important for the history of Jewish coinage, religion, art and folklore. Only incidentally have they been mentioned in numismatics and otherwise, and have not been given the appreciation they deserve. In this study[2] they are treated as a homogeneous group, having a central idea. They depict the beliefs of the people at that period, and are mainly agricultural symbols, connected with the agricultural festivals in the Temple.[3]

[1] A general term, "symbol," for both type and symbol is used in this study.

[2] An address delivered at the Numismatic Society of America, New York City, on March 3rd, 1940. The writer is indebted to its President, Mr. Edward T. Newell, for his kind co-operation in putting his private collection at the writer's disposal and for reading this Ms. Since this study went to press, the untimely passing away of Mr. Newell occurred, which is a great loss to the scholarly world in general and in particular to that of numismatics.

The writer wishes to thank Profs. Albright, Ginzberg and Goodenough for having read the Ms. and for their valuable suggestions. The comments of Prof. Louis Ginzberg are added to the notes of the writer, hereafter cited as Ginzberg.

[3] The writer, as the reader will note, employed extreme brevity because of lack of space. For this reason the texts found in the quoted sources were not copied, and not all the Hebrew quotations were translated. Thus, it is impossible to give the chronology of each source quoted, and in order better to understand the gradual development of the discussed symbols, the reader should keep in mind the period that the rabbinic literature covers, from the tannaitic to some of the midrashic works.

Human and animal types are absent from the Jewish coins. The types used are:

Agricultural: Palm tree;[4] palm branch;[5] lulab;[6] ethrog;[7] vine and grapes; grape leaf; pomegranate, single and buds;[8] lily-rose;[9] cornucopiae; laurel wreath; wreath with olives.[10]

Buildings: Temple.

Astronomical: Menorah; star.[11]

[4] The palm tree is found on Greek coins, especially of Crete and the Aegean Islands. It is also found on non-Jewish coins of Palestine. The palm tree was prominent in Babylon, and even now one of the principal agricultural commodities of Iraq is dates. The palm tree on the Jewish coins does not appear as a sacred tree but as the most characteristic tree of that land. See the chapter: Palm tree.

[5] The palm branch is found on non-Jewish coins as a symbol of victory and honor. On the Jewish coins it represents a ritual, and the palm branch within the wreath on the bronze coins of Bar Kochba seems to be associated with the *Hallel* (see ch. The Lily). The *Hallel* is a song of divine victory and honor. In *Pesikta*, ed. Buber, 180a, the palm branch is explained as a symbol of victory. Ginzberg holds that it is very likely that on the Bar Kochba coins the palm branch is to celebrate the victory of the revolution.

[6] The *lulab* type is, to the writer's knowledge, unique.

[7] The ethrog type seems likewise to be unique, if we should disregard the melon type.

[8] The shape of the three budding pomegranates on the shekels and half-shekels is singular in numismatics.

[9] The rose on the non-Jewish coins seems to be a solar symbol, and the fact that the lily-rose was found on the Menorah and on the Eastern Gate of the Temple (see the chapter: Lily) may suggest such a relationship. The open six-petaled rose on some of the Rhodian coins resembles the rosettes on Jewish ossuaries. The other types of rosettes and their meaning will be discussed separately.

[10] See note 17.

[11] The star type is found on the reverse of some coins of Alexander Jannaeus (Hill, XXII, 1 f.) and as a symbol over the tetrastyle on the tetradrachms of the Second Revolt of Bar Kochba. The star on the Jewish coins is to be regarded as an adopted or a parallel symbol but not alien to the Jews. A Hebrew inscription: "King Jehonathan," is found on some coins between the rays and on others surrounding them.

The most frequent form of star in numismatics consists of eight rays, it being employed in many lands. Its earliest form seems to be the star found on the coins of Itanus, Crete, dating from the 5th–4th cent. B. C. E. (see B. M., *Crete and the Aegean Islands*, Pl. XII, 6–7). It

Utensils: Amphora; ampula; omer-cup;[12] trumpets,[13] lyres.[14]

consists of a circle with eight voluted rays and set within a square. The star on some coins represents the sun, and on others a star.

The star on the coins of Alexander Jannaeus may suggest the morning star or the sun or the heavens. We find the Menorah (q. v.) symbolizing the solar system, and it would not be foreign to have such a symbol on Jewish coins.

The star on the tetradrachms is found over the portico of the tetrastyle. These coins, as the workmanship shows, were made in haste. On some the star resembles a cross, while on others the star is a radiated round object with eight rays. On non-Jewish coins with temple types the pediments have a star or a patera in the center. On the Jewish tetradrachms the pediment is omitted, as according to rabbinic sources and Josephus the façade of the Temple was 100 cubits square and the position of the Ulam did not require a pediment in front (east), as its length ran north and south. The star, suggesting a pedimental star, may have represented celestial abode, as the Temple actually symbolized the world and the Holy of Holies the Seat of Divine Glory.

Ginzberg holds that the star on the Bar Kochba coins is an allusion to the star — Messiah. R. Akiba employed דרך כוכב to refer to Bar Kochba, and is a Jewish adaptation of a well known type.

[12] The omer (cup) appears only on a coin of Simon and on the silver shekels and half-shekels of the First Revolt. The corn was a symbol employed extensively on coins of Asia Minor, Syria and Egypt (see B. M., *The Ptolemies*, 1883, Pl. VIII; B. M., *Catal. of the Greek coins of Phoenicia*, plates XLIX, 2–4; XLIV, 4). The cornucopia, an adopted symbol on Jewish coins, appears first on the reverse of the coins of John Hyrcanus as a dominant motif, and continued during the entire Hasmonean period. It is quite possible that after Simon, the cornucopia was supposed to have represented a general idea of abundance and fertility. The double cornucopiae on the larger coins of John Hyrcanus (Hill, XX, 16) are formed after those found on Syrian and Egyptian coins with the horns filled with corn and grapes and pomegranates or poppies. The details of the cornucopiae on the smaller denominations of John Hyrcanus suggest the same fruits.

The type resembling a cup, as pointed out later, is the omer, its design resembling the Temple laver. The drinking cup, *kantharos*, of Dionysus usually has handles and was shaped differently. The design on the Jewish coins is extremely rare in numismatics. The closest resemblance to the omer is a basin type on the coin of Pergamum (Anson, *Numismata Graeca*, part I, 357). In this respect it parallels the idea of the omer.

[13] The two trumpets are unique in numismatics.

[14] The lyre and *kithara* with the Apollo type are found on Greek coins. The similar instruments on the Jewish coins of Bar Kochba are not

Symbols: Palm branch; ethrog; basket with dates; pomegranate; ark; star.

Conspicuously absent are the wheat, barley,[15] the fig,[16] and olive,[17] species among the choicest fruits of Palestine.

adopted symbols. They were used in the Temple in early times. The shapes of the lyre and *kithara* on the Jewish coins differ slightly from those on non-Jewish coins.

[15] The wheat and barley are incorporated in the omer type, q. v.

[16] Figs were brought to the Temple as first-fruits (M. Bik. 3.1, 3; Tos. Bik. 2.16). The absence of the fig from Jewish coins was perhaps due to the fact that only those living near Jerusalem brought fresh figs and the rest brought them in pressed form. Comp. M. Bik. 3. See, also Yer. Bik. 3.2, 65c: מי שהיו לו בכורים גרוגרות היה מעטרן תאנים, "he who brought his Bikkurim dry figs decorated it with fresh figs." As the first-fruits had been brought from Pentecost on, the figs were not yet ripe and pilgrims could hardly have brought figs during the summer. Cf. M. Shev. 2.5: סכין את הפגים ומנקבין אותם עד ראש השנה. The figs ripened at New Year — Sukkot time. See also Dalman, *Arbeit und Sitte in Palästina*, I, p. 57, 37 f. Most of the figs seem to have been brought after Sukkot when the prescribed recitation was omitted (M. Bik. 1.6). Another possible cause for the omission of the fig as a symbol on Jewish coins was perhaps that the fig tree in the East had the meaning of death and evil. See I. Loew, *Flora*, I, 227 f., 249; Dalman, *Arbeit und Sitte*, I, 57.

Ginzberg holds that the fig was not used as a symbol on coins because the fig tree was identified in the popular belief with the עץ הדעת, the tree of knowledge, the tree that brought death into the world. Cf. Ginzberg, *Legends*, I, 96. (Gen. Rab. 19.11), and Index to *Legends*, s. v. Fig, the forbidden fruit.

Amoraic traditions are that the tree was a vine (Gen. Rab. 19.8) and an ethrog tree (ib. 20.20).

The main period of the pilgrimage to Jerusalem with the first-fruits seems to have been at Sukkot time or somewhat earlier.

[17] The olive as an independent type on Jewish coins is wanting. Since the agricultural symbols represent also Temple gifts, first-fruits, brought during the summer period, from Pentecost to Sukkot, or from harvest to the vintage season, when the standard text from Deuteronomy was recited (M. Bik. 1.6), the olives were not as yet ripe. Cf. Yer. Yeb. 15.2, 14d: יצא בציר ונכנס מסיק, "when the grape-cutting is over, the olive harvest begins." Some early olives, however, were brought as Bikkurim (cf. Tos. Bik. 2.8). Olives, on the other hand, did not remain long in their natural form as they were pressed for making oil. The absence of an olive-branch from Jewish coins could be perhaps attributed to the fact that it was employed on the Athens coins which were in circula-

This study treats of the Jewish types and symbols on the coins, as the Jews themselves understood them, their origin, development and meaning, although some of the types, like the palm, rose, pomegranate, lily, grapes, wreaths, star, and lyre are found on earlier and contemporary non-Jewish coins. Only those that have a direct bearing or influence on the Jewish types are mentioned.

These types and symbols on the Jewish coins, as well as other Jewish symbols, are found on mosaics, paintings, sculptures, ossuaries, and tombstones. These the writer hopes to discuss at a later date as they require separate treatment.

Limitation of space compels utmost brevity. For this reason the author has not presented all Jewish sources in regard to the fuller history and implications connected with these types and symbols, but limited himself to those that have a direct bearing on the subject. For the same reason he has also eliminated the translation of many of the Hebrew quotations.

The types on the Jewish coins are significant in affording a better insight into the psychology of the people in the century before and after the Christian era. They clarify further the understanding of the Jewish festivals and beliefs. The Second Revolt types depict the hope of the Jews after the destruction of their Temple by the Romans. It is evident, as the types and symbols demonstrate, that the Jews, in the main, lived mostly an agricultural and exoteric life. The messianic idea, on the whole, did not yet enter the

tion in Palestine. Ginzberg holds that the olive branch was not used because of its wide use for bridal couples (Yer. Sota 9.16).

According to a passage in Yer. Bik. 3.2, 65c: ועטרת של זית בראשו שהוא ממין שבעה, because the olive was among the seven prominent products of Palestine, a golden olive-wreath was placed upon the head of the ox which the pilgrims took to Jerusalem to be sacrificed when presenting their Bikkurim.

minds of the people. In the early time of Jewish coinage during the rule of the Maccabees, the Sadducees who did not believe in resurrection, were in power. Even when the Pharisees became the ruling party, the messianic idea in the Christian sense was still far from the minds of the people. On the whole, a redeemer was one who fought for the independence of Palestine. Such was Bar Kochba who left a remarkable number of Jewish types by which he illustrated this conception. The types on the Jewish coins invite a deeper study by students of Jewish history and theology.

Chapter II

The symbols on the Jewish coins struck in Palestine[18] cover a period of almost three hundred years, with interludes, from "Simon" Maccabaeus, 139 B. C. E.[19] till the

[18] Before the Maccabean period, in the fourth century B. C. E., there were autonomous Jewish coins in Palestine. See E. L. Sukenik, "The Oldest Coins of Judea," *JPOS*, XIV (1934), 178 f., whose reading of the inscription YHD, Judea, has been commonly accepted; O. R. Sellers, *The Citadel of Beth Zur*, Philadelphia, 1933, p. 33; S. A. Cook, "The Yehu Coin," *ZATW*, LIV (1938), 268 f. In mentioning the historical value of these coins we quote W. F. Albright, *BASOR*, LIII (Feb. 1934), 20 f.:

> "Now we have the compensatory proof that an automous Hebrew silver coinage existed in the fourth century B. C., of which three or four coins are now known. It follows that the Jews were granted theocratic autonomy in the fourth century, under the rule of their high-priests, who received the right to strike their own silver coinage, and to raise their own taxes. After Alexander the Lagides confirmed their privileges, which were not taken away entirely until the conquest of Palestine by the Seleucids."

Since only the inscription, YHD, is Jewish, these coins are not included in the study.

[19] The writer enclosed the name Simon in quotation marks, following the theory advanced by Prof. W. F. Albright that there were no coins of Simon Maccabaeus, or at least none have been found thus far. This is evident both epigraphically and typically. To quote O. R. Sellers and W. F. Albright, "The First Campaign of Excavation at Beth-zur," *BASOR*, XLIII (Oct. 19 31):

end of Jewish coinage in the time of Bar Kochba, 135 C. E. The periods of pure Jewish symbolism on Palestinian coins were three: 1. The Maccabees, 139–37 B. C. E., till Herod

> "A very important by-product of the first campaign at Beth-zur is the definite proof that the bronze coins hitherto ascribed by most numismatists to Simon Maccabaeus cannot belong to him. We have, accordingly, no extant Jewish coins antedating the reign of John Hyrcanus . . . The circumstantial evidence is decisive when we consider that both style and epigraphy point to the First Revolt. All the coins inscribed 'in the fourth year of the redemption of Zion' belong, therefore, to 69/70 A. D."

The symbols on the so-called "Simon" coins belong to the period of the First Revolt, and epigraphically the letters are of a later date than Simon and Hyrcanus. Some letters on the "Simon" coins resemble those on the coins of Antigonus Mattathias, First and Second Revolts, although other letters on the coins of "Simon" fit one or the other of these groups of coinage. On the other hand the symbols on the coins of "Simon" are in closer relation to the period of the two revolts, although they differ in detail as one may see by comparing the "cup" on the bronze coins with the "cup" on the silver shekels and half shekels of the First Revolt, and the *lulab* on the coins of "Simon" with the *lulab* on the silver tetradrachms of the Second Revolt. The Hebrew legend "year four of the redemption of Zion" points to some definite occurrence that continued for almost four years, such as a revolt. This could not apply to Simon. The half and quarter denominations of "year four — half," "year four — quarter" mean bronze half and quarter shekels. In the fourth year of the First Revolt we find half silver shekels. If we assume that the bronze half shekels of "Simon" belong to the period of the First Revolt, it would suggest that in the fourth year the Jews felt a shortage in silver with which to continue the striking of silver half-shekels, and substituted bronze half-shekels. Here again we are faced with the problem of the sudden change of types and symbols on the bronze coins such as the bound *lulab*, *ethrog*, and palm tree with two baskets from those of the former years of the First Revolt. The legends on the bronze coins of "Simon" bearing the inscription לגאלת ציון, "of the redemption of Zion," differ from the legend on the bronze coins of the First Revolt of year two and three which read חרות ציון, "freedom of Zion." If we assume that the "Simon" coins belong to the year four of the First Revolt, they are surely significant and may reflect a definite change in the leadership of the war or a definite religious tendency in the fourth year of the First Revolt against the Romans.

However, as mentioned above, a certain difficulty arises from the fact that although graphically the legends on the coins of "Simon" are closest to those of the First Revolt, the letter *waw* is the same as on

the Great; 2. First Revolt against Rome, 66–70 C. E.; and 3. Second Revolt against Rome, 132–135 C. E.

Some Jewish symbols were to a certain extent employed by Herod I (37–4 B. C. E.);[20] his son Antipas, tetrarch of Galilee and Peraea (4 B. C. E.–39 C. E.);[21] his other son Herod Archelaus, ethnarch of Judea and Samaria (4 B. C. E. –6 C. E.);[22] his grandson Herod Agrippa, ruler of Judea and Samaria (41–44 C. E.);[23] and some of the Roman procurators (6–66 C. E.).[24]

the coins of the Hasmoneans, and the *lamed* is not the same as on the bronze coins of the First Revolt, while the letter *aleph* differs from the *aleph* on the shekels.

Because of these problems the writer followed the order given by F. Hill in the British Museum catalogue, being fully aware of the archaeological facts regarding the so-called coins of "Simon."

In this study the writer discusses the types and symbols on the Jewish coins, their meaning and development. Whether the coins of "Simon" belong to this or that period — as the mentioned problems require further study — does not affect or alter our thesis about the symbols.

If we eliminate the possibility of Simon coins, it becomes evident that true Jewish symbols which have their origin in the Temple on both obverse and reverse of the coins are those belonging to the periods of the two revolts. These coins have only Hebrew inscriptions.

The Maccabees fighting for religious freedom and national independence adopted foreign symbols and Judaized them by eliminating the types found on non-Jewish coins foreign to the Jewish spirit and accepting only the symbols that accompanied these types.

The gradual Hellenization of the Hasmonean family and the Romanization of the Herodian dynasty, the aim of the Jewish revolts, as well as the political changes in Palestine, are vividly portrayed by the types, symbols and inscriptions on the coins.

[20] Pomegranates. Cf. Hill, George Francis. *British Museum: Catalogue of the Greek coins of Palestine*, London, 1914, Pl. XXIV, 1–3. Hereafter cited as Hill.

[21] Palm branch. Hill, XXV, 1–7.

[22] Bunch of grapes. Hill, XXV, 11–12.

[23] Three ears of barley. Hill, XXVI, 1–2.

[24] Ear of barley, Hill, XXVIII, 1–6; three ears of barley, XXIX, 3–4; palm tree, XXVIII, 1–6; XXIX, 13–16; palm branch, XXVIII, 17–20; XXIX, 1–2; two palm branches crossed, XXIX, 11–12; branch of vine, XXVIII, 13–15.

The relationship between the symbols employed by the procurators and the Jewish emblems will be discussed separately.

The non-Jewish symbols on the coins of the various cities and provinces of Palestine represent a record of deities, generals, kings and emperors; of maritime warfare and commercial exploits; of the ploughing under of conquered cities; a gallery of self-glorifying portraits of autocrats, rulers and their wives; of soldiers with spear and helmet trampling upon the bodies of their victims. That is the usual trend of symbolic representation on Palestinian non-Jewish coinage.

In contrast to these are the Jewish symbols depicting a simple faith, symbols in which the hope for a happier life is based upon the blessings received from nature — from God. No human portraits nor animal sacrifices nor pouring of blood upon the altar are to be found among the emblems. The Jewish symbols employed during the three periods of Jewish coinage — the Maccabees and the two revolts — are trees, fruits, flowers, musical instruments and a few ritual objects.

The underlying motif of the Jewish emblems on the ancient Jewish coins in Palestine finds the following expressions:

1. Those of the Maccabean and First Revolt periods are symbols connected with fertility.[25]

2. Of the Second Revolt, besides the symbols of fertility,[26] the Temple itself and a few utensils are represented,[27] prerequisites for the celebration of festivals connected with agriculture and fertility.

3. The early Maccabean symbols represent the offerings of the first-fruits on Passover[28] and Pentecost,[29] and the

[25] Palm tree, palm branch (*lulab*), *ethrog*, baskets with fruits, lily, pomegranate, vine leaf, grapes and vessels for liquids. Hill, XX, XXI, XXX.

[26] Palm tree, *lulab*, grapes and vessels.

[27] Vessels, trumpets and lyre. Hill, XXXIII–XXXVIII.

[28] Cup (omer). Hill, XX, 11–15; XXX, 1–9.

[29] Palm tree with two baskets with fruits — dates. Hill, XX, 8. It is interesting to note the pictorial resemblance between the palm

ceremonies during the Feast of Tabernacles,[30] the three great seasonal-national festivals, attended by multitudes of Jews, both Jerusalemites and pilgrims.[31]

4. The symbols were known to the Jews before the period of Jewish coinage, and some of them were found in the Temple as ornaments on the building and on sacred objects.[32]

5. The above-mentioned emblems were thus Temple symbols.[33]

Palestine, as seen from literature, was an agrarian land, dependent entirely upon the rains during the winter season.[34] The symbols on the coins were taken mainly from the flora, as their physical quality suggested fertility,[35] and

tree with the two baskets (XX, 8) and the *lulab* with the two *ethrogs* (XX, 11, 13) which suggest the graphical similarity of ideas as symbols of fertility.

[30] Lev. 23.40; *lulab* and *ethrog*, Hill, XX, 8–15. See chapters: Lulab and Amphora.

[31] Ex. 34.23: Thrice in the year shall all your men children appear before the Lord God.

[32] Yer. Yoma 4.4 (41d): אמר רבי אחי בר יצחק, בשעה שבנה שלמה את בית המקדש צר כל מיני אילנות לתוכו, R. Aḥi bar Isaac said: when Solomon built the Temple, he fashioned all kinds of trees in it. Jos., *Ant.*, III, 6, 2 (126): This curtain (פרכת) was of great beauty, being bedecked with every manner of flower, plant, that the earth produces. On it were interwowen other designs that could add to its adornment, save the form of living creatures. See also the chapters: Palm, Lily, Pomegranate and Vine.

[33] If not entirely Temple coins, they are to a certain degree hierarchic, as they were struck mainly by priests-rulers, and the types are Temple motifs, or of objects found in the Temple.

[34] Deut. 11.11: But the land, whither ye go to possess it, is a land of hills and valleys, and drinketh water of the rain of heaven. Ibid. 11.17: and he shut up the heaven and there be no rain, and that the land yield not her fruit; and least ye perish quickly . . . Cf. I Kings 17 f.; see also note 51.

[35] E. g., the pomegranate, because it contains numerous seeds. This fruit, besides its other qualities, became a symbol of fertility. The word *zer'a* (זרע) means both seeds and children. Cf. Isa. 1.4; I Kings 11.1; Ezra 9.2; 10.3. See chapter: Pomegranate.

because these fruits and crops were brought to the Temple as offerings. The utensils employed as symbols were used during the ceremonies, suggesting the offerings they contained.

The great agricultural festival held in autumn, on the seventh month,[36] was called *Hag ha-Asif*—Feast of Ingathering.[37] It is also called Sukkot, Feast of Tabernacles or Booths,[38] in which the Jews are supposed to dwell for seven days. This feast ushered in the rainy season.[39] When historical explanations were added to the agricultural festivals, an interpretation was advanced that the *sukkot* or booths are to commemorate the tents in which the Israelites dwelt during their wanderings in the wilderness.[40] The *sukkot* had not been observed since the time of Joshua until after the return from Babylon.[41] The booths were then constructed of twigs, leaves and foliage of olive, pine, myrtle and palm trees.[42] They were more than a reminder of a distant past, but rather a ritual associated with current

[36] Lev. 23.24, 40. Concerning the date of the festival, see J. Morgenstern, "The Calendar of Ancient Israel," *HUCA*, X (1935).

[37] Ex. 24.22; Lev. 23.39.

[38] Lev. 23.24 f.

[39] Mishna R. H. 1.2: בארבעה פרקים העולם נידון: בפסח על התבואה, בעצרת על פירות האילן . . . ובחג נידונין על המים, Judgment is passed upon the world at four seasons: On Passover for crops, on Pentecost for fruits of the tree, and on Ḥag (Sukkot) the sentence of the waters is passed. Cf. M. Ta'an. 1.1: מאמתי מזכירין גבורות גשמים . . . מיום טוב הראשון . . . האחרון של חג.

[40] Lev. 23.42–43.

[41] Neh. 8.17.

[42] Neh. 14.17. In Ezra-Nehemiah times, *sukkot* were erected also in the Temple Court (ibid., 14.16) but not in the Inner Court. Since that practice was connected with fertility rites, the *sukkah* naturally found its place in the Temple area as well, for the use of the priests. As rain was important for the produce of Palestine, people gladly erected *sukkot*, huts, in their own fields and locations to attract the rain-carrying clouds. This ceremony ultimately assumed such proportions that the erection of booths became a home custom, as every farmer wanted to secure enough rain during the winter season.

life and belief.[43] The *sukkah* was a part of the agricultural festival, suggesting fertility and plenty.[44] In later times the leaves and branches that covered the *sukkah* symbolized the heavens and clouds.[45]

The second seasonal festival was Passover when the first-fruits of the new crops of the field,[46] a measure of barley — the Omer,[47] were brought to the Temple as an offering. The third agricultural festival was at the end of this season, on the fiftieth day — Pentecost, when the first-fruits of the grain harvest — two wheat loaves, *bikkurim* — were offered.[48] From then on the first-fruits were brought to the Temple.[49] The last offerings consisted of the seven chief products of Palestine: wheat, barley, grapes, figs, pomegranates, olives and honey (of dates).[50]

[43] Cf. Zech. 14.16–19: Those who will not come up to Jerusalem for Sukkot, the rain will not be upon them.

[44] See preceding notes. Cf. Num. Rab. 11.3: דומה דודי לצבי, מה הצבי הזה מקפץ ממקום למקום ומגדר לגדר ומאילן לאילן מסוכה לסוכה, My beloved is like a gazelle. Just as the gazelle leaps from place to place and from fence to fence and from tree to tree and from hut (*sukkah*) to hut (*sukkah*).

[45] See Targum Onkelos and Jonathan to Lev. 23.42–43: במטלת ענני יקרא, במטלת עננין, *sukkot* denoting clouds. Cf. Mek. of Simon b. Yohai (ed. Hoffmann, p. 40): אין סוכות אלא ענני כבוד, *Sukkot* means the cloud of Divine Presence; Cant. Rab. 2.17: ד"א שמאלו תחת לראשי — זו סוכה, וימינו תחבקני — זה ענן שכינה, "His left hand is under my head" (Cant. 2.6), that means the *Sukkah*, "and his right hand embraces me," that means the cloud of Divine Presence. Also Sifra, Emor, 17.11 (ed. Weiss, p. 103a–b): ר"א אומר סוכות ממש היו, ר"ע — ענני כבוד, R. Eliezer said, the *sukkot* (in the wildness) were actually huts, R. Akiba said, they were clouds of Divine Presence (or glory). On the relation of Divine glory to *Sukkot*, see also H. Torczyner, *Die Bundeslade*, p. 267 f.

[46] The place whence the omer was brought was near Jerusalem. See Paul Romanoff, *Onomasticon of Palestine*, 18.

[47] Lev. 23.9 f.

[48] Ex. 34.22; Lev. 23.15 f.

[49] Ezek. 44.30; Nehem. 10.36; II Chron. 31.5–7.

[50] Deut. 8.8; M. Bik. 1.3.

As rain[51] that causes growth comes from the sea, west of Palestine,[52] that region was regarded as the source of divine blessing and the favorite place of the Lord.[53] In the Temple,

[51] The importance of rain for Palestine and its role in the Jewish ritual, see Paul Romanoff, "Architectural Forms and Symbols of the Temple," *Bodn*, N. Y., 1936, pp. 71–82, 133–158; R. Patai, *HUCA*, XIV (1939), 251 f; D. Feuchtwang, *Das Wasseropfer*, Wien, 1911. See Ps. 65.10–14.

Isa. 55.10: For as the rain that cometh down, and the snow from heaven, and returned not thither, but watereth the earth, and maketh it bring forth and bud, that it may give seed to the sower, and bread to the eater. Rain was considered as the husband (i.e., the fertilizer) of the earth. Ta'an. 6b (based on Isa. 55.10): דאמר רב יהודה מיטרא בעלה דארעא הוא, Rab Judah said: the rain is the husband of the earth. See also the qualifications of rain listed in Ta'an. 6–7. Cf. Cant. Rab. 7.16: ר' יהודה בשם ר' אחא, אין שוקן של גשמים אלא בארץ, the desire of rain is only the earth.

[52] Sifre, Haazinu, s. v. יערף כמטר לקחי (ed. Friedmann, p. 132a): אלא כמטר הזה שבא מן המערב. יערף . . . זה רוח מערבית שהוא ערפו של עולם שכולו לברכה, like the rain that comes from the west which is all for blessing . . . that is the western wind . . . that is all of blessing.

[53] The Shekinah was considered to be in the west. B. B. 25a: דאמר ריב"ל בואו ונחזיק טובה לאבותינו שהודיעו מקום תפילה, דכתיב, וצבא השמים לך משתחוים . . . ור' אבהו אמר שכינה במערב . . . ריב"ל אמר שכינה במערב, R. Joshua b. Levi said, let us be grateful to our ancestors who pointed out to us the direction of prayer, for it is written (Nehem. 9.6): "and the host of heaven worshipeth thee." R. Abahu said, the Shekinah is in the west . . . R. Joshua said, the Shekinah is in the west. Cf. Num. Rab. 2.9: ושכינה לעולם במערב, the Shekinah is always in the west; ibid., 11.3: הנה זה עומד תחת כתלנו, זה כותל מערבי של ביהמ"ק שאינו חרב לעולם, למה שהשכינה במערב, the Western Wall of the Temple will never be destroyed because the glory is in the west. Cf. Sanh. 92b, Yalkut Shim'oni, Neh. 9, the discussion between "Antoninus" and Rabbi. Antoninus asked Rabbi why does the sun set in the west, and Rabbi replied: כדי ליתן שלום לקונה, שנ' וצבא השמים לך משתחוים, in order to offer greetings to the Creator, for it is written (Nehem. 9.6): "and the host of heaven worshippeth thee."

This direction was supplied by the movement of the stars toward the west. Palestine is in a 31′ 30″ latitude. To a person standing in Jerusalem and observing the movement of the heavenly bodies, they seem to move in a somewhat southwesterly direction.

Besides the above, another factor influenced the consideration of the west and southwest as the source of divine power, namely, the rain that comes from these regions which is of vital importance to the land. See notes 34, 51. Cf. also the writer's article ההשתחויות בבית המקדש והפלחן היהודי in *Bitzaron*, March, 1942.

the Holy of Holies was located west of the sanctuary,[54] and the Temple ritual was closely associated with the west.[55]

Jewish coins display the earliest graphically recorded and preserved Jewish symbols. "Simon" Maccabaeus and his followers employed symbols other than the figures of human beings and deities found on the non-Jewish coins. The prerequisite was that the emblems on the Jewish coins were to be understood by the Jews themselves.

The symbols on the coins of "Simon" (143–136 B. C. E.) are, as it will be shown later, associated with nature and produce. They are:[56]

1. *Ethrog* between two *lulabs*.[57]

[54] See the chapter on the Menorah.

[55] The Temple ritual was influenced by the western and southwestern orientation (see note 53). The Holy of Holies was in the west of the sanctuary. The pouring of the sacrificial blood upon the foundation of the altar and the water-libation was on the western corner and horn. The animals, when being slaughtered, had to face south and their heads turned to the west. The priests performing the sacrifices also had to face west. The ascending of the altar-ramp with the offerings ended on the western side (Zeb. 63b; Men. 19b), and for water-libation both the ascending and descending had to be on the western side of the ramp (Tos. Zeb. 7.7): כל העולין למזבח עולין במזרח ויורדין במערב, בימין ויורדין בשמאל, חוץ מניסוך המים והיין ועולת העוף שעולין במערב ויורדין במערב, בימין ויורדין בימין (read: בשמאל ויורדין בשמאל). On the Day of Atonement (M. Yoma 3.5), when the High-priest presented the sin-offering, he had to face the west — the sanctuary, and the bull faced south and its head was turned west. The two goats on the same day had likewise to face west (ibid., 6.2–3). During the sacrifice of the Red Heifer (M. Parah 3.9; Tos. Parah 3.9; Yoma 16a: (ר' אלעזר בן יעקב אומר, כבש עושין לה, לפרה שהיתה עולה בה, ראשה בדרום ופניה במערב), the heifer stood in a similar direction, and the priest who burned it had to face west. While laying on of the hands upon the sacrifice (סמיכה) during confession, both the sacrifice and the offerer had to face west (Tos. Men. 10.12: כיצד סומך. זבח עומד בצפון ופניו למערב, סומך במערב ופניו במערב).

The burning of incense was likewise done on the southwestern side of the altar. Cf. M. Middot 3.1; Tos. Zeb. 6.8, 10; Sifra, Zav 30.3; Zeb. 54a.

[56] Hill, XX, 8–15.

[57] Narkiss, *Coins of Palestine*, Part I, p. 63, holds that to the Hasmoneans the *lulab* and *ethrog* were a symbol of the dedication of the Temple.

2. Palm tree and two baskets of fruit.

3. Two *lulabs*.

4. *Lulab* with two *ethrogs*.

5. Cup.

These could be reduced to three symbols:

1. *Lulab* and *ethrog*.

2. Palm tree with two baskets of fruit.

3. Cup.

Each of these three symbols represented a different festival. The first represented Sukkot, the second Pentecost, the third Passover.

These coins, however, were struck long after its dedication, while the *lulab* and *ethrog* were used on Sukkot. The Temple to be dedicated in the future figures on the tetradrachms of the Second Revolt where the Temple itself is represented.

SECTION TWO

CHAPTER III

PALM AND PALM BRANCH

The palm, a fruit-bearing tree, growing near water,[58] had already in biblical times been synonymous with height and abundance.[59] The sight of such a tree meant the presence of water, an ever-ready meal and rest in its shade.[60] This tree became the symbol of Judea where palm trees grow in greater number than in any other part of Palestine. It also represented Judea the productive, Judea the blessed, and the palm motif figured prominently on the walls, doors and pillars of the Tabernacle and the Temple.[61] The Temple, according to one story, was supposed to have been built in a palm-grove, the City of Palms — Jericho.[62] The palm tree has thus a double meaning, the symbol of Judea and the symbol of abundance and plenty. As symbols have

[58] Ex. 15.27; Nu. 33.9. See I. Loew, Flora, II, p. 306–362.

[59] Cant. 7.8; Ps. 92.13. The palm as symbol of fertility and loftiness figures often on Jewish illuminated marriage contracts.

[60] See note 58.

[61] I Ki. 6.29, 32; 7.36; Ez. 40.16 f.; 41.18 f.; II Chr. 3.5; Jos., Ant. III, 6, 126.

[62] Abot d'r. Nathan 35. See also Deut. 34.3; II Chr. 28.15; Ju. 1.16; 3.13.

the tendency of ever spreading, the palm, in time, became the symbol of Palestine. The palm tree symbolizing Judea is illustrated on the *Judea Capta* coins.[63] The palm tree has also become an emblem of Israel.[64]

Growing near water, lofty, nearer to the clouds than any other tree, the branches were regarded as able to attract the water from heaven, and in the course of time the palm branch was considered to possess the power of attracting rain.[65] The palm branch — the *lulab* — was therefore used in the Temple during the autumn festival, Sukkot, when the ritual of water-libation was performed.[66] It was bound with branches of myrtle and willow.[67] The waving of the lulab in different directions during the ceremony was aimed at gathering the winds that carry the clouds from the four corners of the earth, and from heaven above down to the earth.[68] The myrtle and willow, both grown in the prox-

[63] Hill, XXXI.

[64] Esther Rabbah 9: דקל אמר, אני אתן את עצמי, שבי נמשלו ישראל, שנ' זאת קומתך דמתה לתמר . . . צדיק כתמר יפרח, the palm tree said: I am ready to serve that purpose (as gallows for Haman), for Israel is compared to me . . . b. Sanh. 93a: אמרתי אעלה בתמר, אלו ישראל, I will go up to the palm tree (Cant. 7.9), that means Israel.

[65] Frazer, The magic art, 'The magical control of rains.'

[66] In talmudic literature the term *lulab* is likewise applied to branches in general. Cf. M. Sheviit, 7.5: לולבי זרדים והחרובין . . . לולבי האלה והבטנה והאטודין; M. Orlah 1.7: העלים והלולבים ומי גפנים. The *lulab*, branch of the lofty palm, is found in poetry as a metaphor for children. Cf.: ידיעות המכון לחקר השירה העברית בירושלים, כרך ה', 1939, עמ' 89, לשבת וחתן: לולבים כשתי אחיות יפריחו.

[67] See Targum Onkelos and Jonathan to Lev. 23.40 f.: פרי אלנא (משבח) אתרוגין ולולבין והדסין וערבין (דמרביין על נחלין) דנחל. Cf. b. Ta'an. 2b: וכשם שארבע מינין הללו אי אפשר בהם בלא מים, כך א"א לעולם בלי מים, as these four kinds (palm branch, myrtle, willow, and *ethrog*) need water for growth, so does the world need it to exist. Jos., Ant. III, 10, 4; Maimonides I, הלכות לולב, XII.1 f.; VII, 9.10; Tur, הלכות לולב, 651.

[68] Sukkah 37b; Men. 62a: מוליך ומביא מעלה ומוריד; מוליך ומביא למי שהרוחות שלו, מעלה ומוריד למי שהשמים והארץ שלו. במערבא מתנן . . . מוליך ומביא כדי לעצור רוחות רעות, מעלה ומוריד כדי לעצר טללים רעים. אמר רבא וכן לולב, R. Johanan explained that waving (of the two breads; and the same with the *lulab*) to and fro is in honor of Whom the

imity of water, were attached to the *lulab*. The *ethrog* —

winds appertain, and up and down to Whom are heaven and earth. In Palestine, R. Jose b. Hanina interpreted that one waves to and fro in order to restrain harmful winds; up and down, in order to restrain harmful dew. See also Mekilta of Simon b. Yohai (ed. Hoffmann, p. 40): ויסעו מסכת... אין סכות אלא ענני כבוד... וה' הולך, מלמד ששבעה ענני כבוד היו שם עם ישראל... ארבעה מארבע רוחות, ואחד מלמעלה ואחד מלמטה ואחד שמקדים לפניהם, Sukkot means the clouds of Divine Presence ... Seven clouds of Divine Presence accompanied the Israelites ... four from the four sides, one from above, one from below, and one before them.

The תנופה, waving, was practiced with the Omer and the two breads (Lev. 23). The *lulab* as such is not mentioned in the Bible. It is connected with Sukkot and water-libation, and resembled the ritual associated with the winds and rain, and for that reason the *lulab* was waved like the Omer and the two breads. Cf. Ta'an. 2b: מאמתי מזכירין על הגשמים, רבי אליעזר אומר משעת נטילת לולב, רבי יהושע אומר משעת הנחתו. א"ר אליעזר הואיל וארבע' מינין הללו אינן באין אלא לרצות על המים, וכשם שארבע מינין הללו אי אפשר בהם בלא מים, כך א"א לעולם בלי מים, When do we begin to make mention of rain? R. Eliezer says: from the time of taking the *lulab*; R. Joshua says, from the time the *lulab* is discarded (on the seventh day of Sukkot). Said R. Eliezer: since these four kinds (palm branch, myrtle, willow, and *ethrog*) are intended only to make intercession for water, and as these four kinds cannot grow without water so the world too cannot exist without water. See also Pes. of R. Kah., p. 70a, s. v. תנופה; Lev. Rabbah 30.12: ועכשיו שאמרתי לכם, ולקחתם ביום הראשון, כדי לזכותכם כדי שאוריד לכם מטר, when I told you 'Ye shall take you on the first day,' it is in order to make you worthy of divine favor, so that I may bring down rain for you. See ch. 2 note 26.

Ginzberg remarks that the Mishna (Sukkah 3.7) uses the word נענע meaning 'shaking' and not waving. He holds therefore that the 'waving' of the *lulab* is a later practice, and the motions employed is patterned after the waving, תנופה, of the sacrifices, and which have no connection with water.

The difference between the Omer, the two breads and the *lulab* lies in the fact that the first two were Temple offerings, and with the destruction of the Temple they were discontinued. The *lulab*, not a public offering but an individual matter as was the Sukkah, although used in the Temple, continued to be employed after the destruction. The first two objects could be and were waved. The *lulab*, consisting of four species and held in both hands, could not have been waved the same way as the Omer and the two breads. The waving was actually done with the *lulab* (palm branch) tip. This amounts to 'shaking,' and that is the term found in the Mishna, but explained later that 'shaking' equals 'waving.' The rabbinic sources stress that the 'waving' of the *lulab* was modeled after the waving of the Omer and the two breads as mentioned in the Bible, and no mention is made that it was patterned after the waving of sacrifices, although the latter too were waved.

citron — grown near water,[69] was used during the same ceremony. The palm branch was used in religious processions,[70] and also symbolized dignity, royal honor, jubilation and victory.[71]

Chapter IV

Lulab and Baskets

The bronze shekel of "Simon" Maccabaeus[72] has on the obverse two *lulabs*, in bundles, with citron (*ethrog*) between them. On the reverse is a palm tree with a basket on each side into which dates are falling from the tree.

This emblem on the reverse symbolizes the second kind of offering of the first-fruits, the *Bikkurim*,[73] which began on Pentecost and continued throughout the summer and ended at Sukkot,[74] the original Feast of Ingathering, and even lasted till Hanukkah.[75] The biblical meaning of *Bikkurim* was the offering of the two breads of wheat flour.[76] But in the Second Commonwealth the two breads assumed a

[69] Y. Shab. 3.5 (53d): אמר רבי תנחומא, תרגם עקילס, הדר—הידור, אילן שהוא גדל על פני מים, R. Tanhuma said, Aquila translated Hadar (Lev. 23.40) ὕδωρ, a tree that grows near water.

The *ethrog* is symbolic of Israel. See Lev. Rabba, Emor, 30.10–11, and Nu. Rabbah 4.21.

[70] I Macc. 13.37; Lev. Rabbah, Emor, 30.13: שתי כפות תמרים להלל בהן, two palm branches for the recitation of Hallel (Praise).

[71] II Macc. 14.4; II Esdras 2.45.

[72] Hill, XX, 8.

[73] Ex. 23.19; 34.26; Nu. 18.13; Deut. 26.1–11; Philo, On the festival of the basket of first-fruits; On humanity, X. See also Cant. Rabbah 2.27: התאנה חנטה פגיה, אלו הסלים של בכורים.

[74] M. Bikk. 1.6, 10; Philo, On the festival of the basket, III.

It seems that the main stream of pilgrims came at that time. See chapter: String instruments. See also Joseph Hochman, Jerusalem Temple Festivals.

[75] M. Bikk. 1.6.

[76] Lev. 23.15–20.

new interpretation and began to signify the first-fruits of the garden, which were brought in baskets and presented to the Temple where they were placed at the altar. The offerings were later distributed among the priests.[77] The emblem on the coins of Simon shows that the bringing of fruits to the Temple had long been in practice, and it continued till the last days of the Temple. A vivid description of the procession bearing the first-fruits is recorded in the Mishna:[78] All the people of the towns and villages, with their fruits, gather in the leading town of the district and camp in the open places, not entering the houses. In the morning the deputy calls: 'Arise, let us go up to Zion, to the House of our Lord.' Those nearest to Jerusalem bring figs and grapes, and those from afar bring dry figs and raisins. An ox, to be sacrificed, steps in front of them, and its horns are covered with gold, and an olive crown is placed on its head. The flutists precede, playing, until they reach Jerusalem. When they near Jerusalem, they send out messengers announcing their coming. Then they decorate their *Bikkurim* with additional fruits, not of the seven kinds. The grandees, the chiefs and the treasurers of the Temple come out to meet them. The reception is according to the importance of the approaching pilgrims. The artisans of Jerusalem stand along the road greeting them: 'Brethren, people of that and that place, we greet you.' The flutists precede, playing until they reach the Temple ground. Then each in procession takes a basket on his shoulder, and marches until he reaches the *Azarah* (Inner Court). In the *Azarah* the Levites begin to sing: 'I will extol thee, O Lord . . .'[79] On top of the baskets were placed pigeons to be sacrificed, and the fruits were

[77] Nu. 18.13; Ex. 44.30; II Chr. 31.4–6. Philo, The special laws, I, XXVII, 133 f.

[78] M. Bikk. 3.2–8. Philo, On the festival of the basket, III.

[79] Ps. 30.2.

given to the priests. While the baskets are still on their shoulders, the people recite two verses from Deuteronomy 26.3–4, then they lower the baskets and hold on to the brims, while the priests put their hands under the baskets and lift them up a little, and recite from verse 5 to the end of the chapter. Then the pilgrims placed the baskets near the altar, and bowing, departed. The wealthy bring their *Bikkurim* in baskets of silver and gold, and the poor in twined baskets of reed. Both the baskets and the fruits are given to the priests.

The palm tree on the coin is generic, and represents the finest and most useful tree, one of the seven choicest plants of Palestine. The dates also signify honey,[80] a biblical metaphor for bounty.[81] Thus the reverse of the coin representing the palm and two baskets full of dates symbolizes abundance and plenty.

Chapter V

Cup — Omer

The "cup" appears on the reverse side of the bronze coins of Simon the Hasmonean and on the obverse of the silver Shekels and half Shekels of the First Revolt.[82] This vessel has been identified as a cup or chalice[83] or the cup of manna.[84] It is doubtful whether or not the vessel was a drinking cup. The dotted border would make drinking

[80] Deut. 8.8; 26.9, 15; M. Bikk. 1.10. The honey mentioned in the Bible is usually the honey of dates in the Talmud. Cf. b. Sukkah 6a; y. Bikk. 1.3. See also Rashi to Deut. 26.2, and b. Ber. 41b, s. v. דבש.

[81] Deut. 7.3.

[82] Hill, XX, 11–15; XXX, 1–9.

[83] Hill, pp. 185 and 269: chalice; Madden, p. 67: cup or chalice; Narkiss, pp. 96 and 118: גביע — cup; Anson, Greek coin types, 3, XXV, 1408 — chalice.

[84] Madden, p. 70.

almost impossible. The cup, '*kos*', in the Temple was used for sacrificial blood;[85] while the drinking of wine in the Temple was forbidden,[86] and as mentioned above, the Jewish coins do not contain any symbol of blood sacrifices.[87] The drinking of a cup of wine was not known in the Jewish Temple ritual in the time of the Maccabees or of the First Revolt, immediately before the destruction of the Temple.[88] Wine was only poured on the altar.[89] On the reverse of the bronze coins of the First Revolt, years two and three, there is found a vine branch with a leaf. The wine as a distinct symbol is recognized on these coins by the vine leaf and by the cluster of grapes on the coins of the Second Revolt.[90] This would eliminate the possibility of the vessel being a chalice. As mentioned above, the symbols on the coins of Simon the Hasmonean are not associated with the ritual to which the libation of wine belonged, but were specifically used during the three main festivals. The

[85] M. Tamid 3.1: השקו את התמיד בכוס של זהב, the Tamid was given to drink from a golden cup (kōs). Cf. also M. Zeb. 8.6: כוס בכוסות; ib. 8.8: חטאת שקבל דמה בשתי כוסות.

[86] Jer. 35.

[87] See *JQR*, XXXIII, 1942.

[88] The benediction over wine is a home custom and late. It seems to have originated before the destruction of the Temple. See Ber. 50b–51a; M. Ber. 6.1; M. Pes. 10.1–8. Book of Jubilees 49, 6–7. The priests were forbidden to drink wine in the Temple.

[89] Lev. 23.37; Nu. 15.4 f.; 28.1 f. Narkiss, op. cit., p. 63: the cup on the coins symbolizes the wine-libation in the Temple. He assumes that the cups on the table of the Arch of Titus represent this same cup. These cups, however, were not for wine but for frankincense. Cf. Jos., Ant. III, 6, 6 (143); ib., III, 10, 5 (182); M. Men. 11.3: שני בזיכין לבונה.

Ginzberg holds that it is quite plausible that the cup symbolized the wine-libation which not only was brought with almost all sacrifices — private and public — but which could be brought by itself.

The thesis of this paper, as the writer shows, is that the coin-types do not represent sacrifices, but merely agriculture, the ritual connected with it, and the sanctuary.

[90] Hill, XXX, 11–15 (vine branch with leaf); XXXIII, 7, 8, 14, 15; XXXIV, 1–3, 20; XXXV, 1–13. See the chapter: Vine and Grapes.

'chalice', or 'cup', rather signifies the golden vessel that contained the Omer and was used on the second day of Passover when a measure of barley, a tenth of an *ephah*,[91] equal to one and a half pints[92] of fine flour, was offered to the Temple as the first-fruits of the field.[93] The waving of this vessel in different directions during the offering corresponded to the waving of the *lulab*.[94] The Omer was also interpreted as having an effect upon the winds that attracted the clouds during the rainy season, and dispersed them in summer,[95] when rain was considered harmful, especially during the harvest period.[96]

It is worthwhile noticing that the symbols found on the coins of Simon: the lulab, palm tree, *ethrog* and baskets — eliminating for a moment the so-called chalice — are mentioned in the Bible and in tannaitic literature. The object that has been considered to be a chalice is not mentioned

[91] Ex. 16.36. This would equal an עשרון. Although a vessel named עשרון was used daily during sacrifices of the Tamid, it was used mainly for measuring purposes (Nu. 29–29). The Omer, however, had nothing to do with the function of the עשרון, and the Omer was a seasonal offering. See also the preceding note.

[92] Cf. Jos., Ant. III, 6, 6 (142): two assarons = seven Attic cotylae (= 3½ pints; one assaron = 1¾ pints).

[93] Lev. 23.10. Jos., Ant. V, 1.4, says that when the Israelites crossed the Jordan and camped near Jericho, they celebrated Passover amid plenty, for they reaped the corn of the Canaanites, which was then ripe, and the Manna stopped.

[94] Lev. 23.11; Pesikta of R. Kahana, p. 70a, s. v. תנופה; Rashi to Lev. 23.11; b. Men. 62a.

[95] Pes. of R. Kahana, p. 69a: ואני משיב לך רוחות ומעלה גשמים וטללים ומגדל צמחים . . . ואין אתם מביאין לי את העומר, and I cause the winds to blow for you and bring up rains and dews and cause plants to grow . . . and you do not bring me the Omer; Eccl. Rabbah 1.4: והקב"ה מוציא מעט רוח ומנגב את הארץ, ואין אנו נותנין לו אלא העומר בלבד, and God brings forth a slight wind and dries the earth, and we offer him only the Omer. See also Pes. of R. Kahana, p. 70a; Nu. Rabbah 12.12: ומנין שהרוחות צורך התבואה, שכן כתיב: יערף כמטר לקחי, and how do we know that the grain needs the winds, for it is written: My doctrine shall drop as the rain.

[96] I Sam. 12.17–19.

as such in any of these sources. When we consider this vessel as the Omer, and a measure by that name did exist,[97] we find its symbolism in the Bible. No sufficient reason was given by writers on this subject for the particular shape of the chalice or cup, with its dotted rim and the two dots underneath it as it appears on the shekel and half-shekel of year one, of the First Revolt.[98]

The interpretation of the meaning of the Omer and *Bikkurim* given in the tannaitic sources,[99] which reflect the concepton of late temple times, does not agree with the Bible. In Leviticus 23, the only place where the offering of the Omer is mentioned, the dates for its offering and of the *Bikkurim* are not set or defined.[100]. The first offering had to be made at the beginning of the harvest and the other, fifty days later. The exact days and months when the offerings had to be brought, as in the case of the other festivals, are not stated. The Pharisaic law defined the bringing of the Omer on the second day of Passover, and *Bikkurim*, fifty days later, on the festival of Pentecost.[101] The offering of the Omer had no connection with Passover or the Exodus, and the offering of the *Bikkurim* had no relation to the Revelation on Mt. Sinai supposed to have occurred on Pentecost.[102]

[97] Ex. 16.36; Lev. 23.10 f.; b. Men. 89b. Sifra, Emor, 10.5 (ed. Weiss, p. 100c): שלשה שמות יש לו: עומר שבלים, עומר תנופה, עומר שמו, the Omer has three names: Omer of the barley, waving omer, and Omer as such. Cf. Jos., Ant. VIII, 3, 8; M. Men. 6.4, 5; ib. 10.1. The Omer, an Assaron, consisted of three Saa, cf. M. Men. 7.7: העומר בא עשרון, משלש סאין.

[98] Madden, p. 67, note 2: the pellets, as well as those round the rim are intended to represent the jewels of the golden chalice of the Temple (Jos., Ant. XII, 2, 10). Josephus, however, does not describe chalices but bowls — craters, see ed. Niese.

[99] See note 103.

[100] Nu. 28.26 f.; Deut. 16.9 f.

[101] B. Shab. 86b; Yoma 4b. These tannaitic (Pharisaic) sources quote two traditions as to the day the Ten Commandments were given: the sixth and seventh of the third month.

[102] See preceding note.

The interpretation found in the tannaitic literature is that the Omer was offered so that the crops in the field might be blessed, and the *Bikkurim* — the two loaves of wheat bread — so that the fruits of the garden might be blessed. This differs from the Priestly Code which does not mention the garden fruits at all.[103]

[103] Tos. Sukkah 3.15; ib. Rosh Hash. 1.12–13; Sifre (ed. Friedman, p. 55a); b. Rosh. Hash. 16a; y. Rosh. Hash. 1.3 (57b): א"ר עקיבא, אמרה תורה, הבא שעורים (עומר) בפסח מפני שהוא פרק שעורים (תבואה) שתתברך עליך תבואה (שבשדות); הבא חיטים (בכורים; ב' הלחם) בעצרת שהוא פרק חיטים (אילן) שיתברכו עליך פירות האילן; נסך מים בחג שהוא פרק גשמים כדי שיתברכו עליך גשמים (גשמי ברכה; גשמי שנה), R. Akiba said: the Torah ordained that you bring barley (var.: the Omer) on Passover because it is the season of barley (var.: crop), so that the crop (var.: the crop of the field) may be blessed; bring wheat of Bikkurim (var.: Bikkurim; the two breads) on Azeret which is the season of the wheat (var.: trees; fruits of the trees), so that the fruit of the trees may be blessed; libate water on Ḥag which is the season of rains, so that the rains (var.: the rains of the year; blessed rains) may be blessed.

SECTION THREE

Chapter VI

Cornucopia

A SYMBOL that made its appearance on Jewish coins immediately after "Simon," 135 B. C. E., and continued on the coins of the Maccabees and in a lesser degree on the coins of the Herodian dynasty, is the double cornucopia and in a few instances the single cornucopia.[104]

The cornucopia, when appearing alone, without the goddesses Copia or Demeter, were abstract symbols. In this respect the horns of plenty were akin to the Jewish symbols. The cornucopia and the palm-tree and palm-branch were symbolically related. The myth connected with the horn of Achelous, the son of Oceanus who was the representative of all fresh waters, perhaps resembles Ridya, the angel of rain, sometimes assuming the form of an ox, in Jewish mythology.[105]

[104] Hill, XX, 16–21; XXI, f.; XXII, 13–18; XXIII, 1–10; XXIV, 9–11; XXV, 8–10; XXVI, 8; XXVII, 10, 12, 16.

[105] B. Ta'an. 25b: אמר רבה, לדידי חזי לי האי רידיא דמי לעגלא . . . וקיימא בין תהומא תתאה לתהומא עילעא. See Rashi, ad. loc.: מלאך הממונה על הגשמים, the angel in charge of rain. Cf. Yoma 21a: ת״ר שלש קולות הולכין מסוף העולם ועד סופו, ואלו הן: קול גלגל חמה . . . וי״א אף רידייא, and Rashi: מלאך הממונה על השקות הארץ ממטר השמים ממעל ומן התהום מתחת . . . ולכן נקרא רידייא לשון שור החורש. See also Ginzberg, *Geonica*, II, p. 345. In geonic times the same explanation was accepted.

The symbol of plenty on the coins of Simon was the palm, palm-branch, baskets with fruits, and the Omer (cup). These symbols disappear from the coins of Johanan Hyrcanus and his successors to be resumed only at the First Revolt, when national spirit was at its height. The absence of earlier symbols on the coins after Simon can be explained by the gradual hellenization of the Hasmonean family, by the appearance of lengthy inscriptions on the fields of the coins, and for political reasons. With the growth of the Jewish state during the rule of Johanan and his successors, and Jewish coinage gaining recognition, and to aid Jewish trade, a symbol like the cornucopia was adopted. This symbol having the same meaning as the two baskets of fruits on the coins of Simon was understood by the nations around Palestine.

Chapter VII

Vessels for Liquids

Four kinds of vessels for liquids are among the symbols on the coins struck by the Jews:[106] 1. The vessel on the coins of "Simon" and on the shekels and half-shekels of the First Revolt,[107]— regarded to be a cup, and identified now as the Omer; 2. The narrow-necked amphorae, covered and uncovered, and with angular handles on the bronze coins of the First Revolt;[108] 3. The one-handled ampula on the silver denarii of the Second Revolt;[109] 4. The amphora on the large bronze coins of the Second Revolt.[110]

[106] The vessels on the coins of the Procurators are not discussed here.
[107] Hill, XX, 11–15; XXX, 1–9.
[108] Hill, XXX, 11–15, 16.
[109] Hill, XXXVIII, 5, 6, 9, 10, 14, 15; XXXIV, 4–10.
[110] Hill, XXXV, 14; XXXIV, 1–3, 10.

The purpose of the vessels has not been established nor their usage.[111] Although the intervals of time between the revolts have to be accounted for, it is evident from their shape and size that each vessel might have contained a different kind of liquid. Considering them from the symbolic point of view, we shall be able to ascribe to them the proper liquids, and their usage in the ritual, as it was pointed out in the beginning of this discussion that all emblems on the coins were used in the Temple.[112]

CHAPTER VIII

AMPULA OR HYDRIA ON THE SILVER DENARII

The two main festivals, the Feast of Tabernacles and Passover, as seen from Jewish literature, are connected with the autumnal and vernal equinoxes respectively.[113] They are at the same time connected with the agricultural festivals.[114] The autumn-festival was also known for the 'water-libation' as a medium of producing rain. This festival was celebrated when the moon was full, the night of the second day of *Sukkot* or Tabernacles,[115] and regarded as the most joyous occasion of the year.[116] It was marked

[111] Narkiss, p. 64: the כד (amphora) on the coins of the First and Second Revolts are symbols of production of Palestine; this is also the symbol of the miracle of the cruse of oil.

[112] See p. 2.

[113] B. Erub. 56a; Rashi to Rosh Hash. 24a, s. v. כאן בימות החמה. Lev. Rabbah, Emor, 26.4: תניא, באחד בתקופת ניסן ובאחד בתקופת תשרי היום והלילה שוין. On the first of the cycle of Nisan (vernal equinox) and on the first of the cycle of Tishri (autumnal equinox) the day and night are even. Philo VII, *The Special laws I*, 181,186; ib. II, XXXIII, 204.

[114] Lev. 23.10, 39; Deut. 16.1, 13. Philo, ib., 172.

[115] M. Sukkah 5.2.

[116] Ib., 5.2. Regarding the term בית השואבה see Joseph Hochman, Jerusalem Temple Festivals, p. 54 f.; E. Epstein, *Tarbitz*, p. 135 f.; S. Lieberman, *Kirjath Sepher*, XII, p. 56; Feuchtwanger, MGWJ, LIV, 45.

by the drawing of three measures of water from the Pool of Siloam in a golden jar. Amidst a great procession and ceremony the water was poured out on top of the altar.[117] Water was poured on each of the seven days of the holiday at morning sacrifices.[118] The festivity of the 'drawing-of-water,' known for the accompanying illumination, as it was celebrated at night, surpassed all bounds.[119] Tradition has it that all Jerusalem was illumined by the light from the Temple,[120] and Josephus, an eye-witness, states that it was a blaze of illumination.[121]

The water-libation, besides the *lulab*, was connected with the season, and was a form of sympathetic magic to induce abundance of rain during the winter-season needed for the crops of Palestine.[122] Such an agricultural festival was no doubt known to every Jew irrespective of whether he was living in Palestine or in the Diaspora. The symbol of water-libation, the celebration of abundance, was the pouring of water from a golden vessel.[123] This is the

[117] Ib., 5.2: At the close of the first festival day on the Feast, they went down to the Court of Women, where they made a great amendment . . .; M. Suk. 4.5.

[118] M. Suk. 4.1.

[119] Ib., 5.2.

[120] Ib., 5.2.

[121] *Against Apion.* II, 118.

[122] See ch. *Omer*, note 22. Cf. b. Ta'an. 25b and B. B. 151b: א"ר אליעזר כשמנסכין את המים בחג, תהום אומר לחברו, אבע מימיך, קול רעים אני שומע, R. Eliezer said: When water-libation is performed, one *t'hom* says to the other (upper depth to the lower depth), let thy waters spring forth, I hear friendly noises (the water and wine libations). According to Sukkah 48a, the water was poured in a dish on top of the south-western horn, and through a hollow it reached the תהום under the altar.

[123] M. Suk. 4.5. The vessel for water libation was called צלוחית, *Zloḥit*, (M. Yoma 2.4; M. Shek. 6.2. M. Meila 3.8; y. M. Suk. 4.7; Tos. Suk. 3.3. Cf. also M. Parah 9.1). The same name was applied to the vessel that contained the oil of instalation (Tos. Shek. 2.18; Yoma 2.7; Sota 13.1; b. Shek. 22a); was attached to the belt of the priest a vessel with oil for the kindling of the Menorah (Yer. Sab.

ampula (lekythos) or hydria, a narrow-necked jug with one handle and fluted body, found on the silver denarii of the Second Revolt.[124] The purpose of this vessel for water-libation on *Sukkot* is borne out by the presence of a palm-branch that is found to the right of the ampula. Both of them were used on *Sukkot* and with the same aim.[125] In this way the symbols complement each other. The reason for employing this vessel as a symbol is also borne out by contemporary tannaitic literature. Since the destruction of the Temple, the people complained that the rains upon which the welfare of Palestine depended, were not blessed and did not come at the proper time,[126] as without the altar, libations could not be performed. In this symbol Bar Kokba pointed out that the rebuilding of the Temple and the renewal of the ritual would bring abundance once more.

The vessels on the bronze coins of the First Revolt do not have the attribute of the palm-branch as in the case of the ampula. They are amphorae,[127] one with angular handles.[128] The difference in time between the two revolts, 65 years, has to be considered, as it is impossible to expect the same forms of vessels as on the coins already discussed. The amphorae are of two kinds, and they were, therefore, used for at least two of the three liquids: water, wine and oil. A few amphorae have lids.[129] The story of the sealed cruse of oil of Hanukkah is late and

10.3, 12c; Nu. Rab. 4, end); and for other purposes in the Temple (Zeb. 80a; M. Zeb. 11.1). They all refer to a small vessel containing from one to three measures, and used mainly both for water and oil.

[124] Hill XXXIII, 5, 6, 9, 10, 14, 15; XXXIV, 4–10, 20.

[125] See Rashi to Yoma 26b, s. v. באחרוגיהן: ללמדנו שניסוך המים אינו אלא בשעת נטילת לולב, water-libation is when the lulab is taken.

[126] See ch. XI, Second Revolt, note 159.

[127] Hill, XXX, 11–16.

[128] Hill, XXX, 16.

[129] Hill, XXX, 12.

not of Palestinian origin.[130] From mishnaic sources we learn that only two liquids, water and wine, usually required covers.[131] Since none of the emblems of this period suggest the Menorah, the amphorae were either for water or wine, both used for libation during Sukkot. As water libation at that time was an established ritual, one of the amphorae was definitely used for that purpose.

Chapter IX

Amphora

The single-handled ampula on the denarii of the Second Revolt suggested as hydria for water-libation, the other vessels remain to be identified. They are the amphorae.[132] To the same period of the Second Revolt, as the ampula, belongs the amphora with the fluted body on the large bronze coins bearing the inscription 'Jerusalem' or '*Shim'on Nasi Yisrael.*'[133]

Three kinds of liquids were used in the Temple: water, wine and oil. Water and wine were used for libation.[134] Oil was used for the meal-offerings, the weekly breads, the bread eaten by the priests, for lighting, and especially of the *Menorah* for which purest oil was prepared.[135] In following our thesis that all symbols on the coins were of objects used in the Temple and for most important occasions and purposes, only vessels that contained the three liquids have to be considered, and not the many other vessels directly connected with the sacrifices, as mixing-

[130] Zeitlin, Hanukkah, *JQR*, 1939, p. 11, correctly pointed out that Palestinian sources did not know of the legend of oil.

[131] M. Ter. 8.4; M. Suk. 4.5; M. Parah 11.1; b. Hul. 10a.

[132] Hill, XXX, 11–16.

[133] Hill, XXXV, 14; XXXVI, 1–3, 10.

[134] M. Sukkah 4.5; b. Suk. 49b; Nu. 15.5 f.

[135] Ex. 27.20.

bowls, bowls, jars, cups, simpuli, etc.; nor the large storage jars-amphorae for wine and oil found in the Temple, but those actually used in the ritual.

From the time of Antigonus Mattathias[136] till the Second Revolt, 175 years had passed. After the destruction of the Temple the symbol of the Menorah was too sacred to be reproduced on coins. That was due perhaps to the memory which sponsored the prohibition of not reproducing the seven-branched *Menorah*,[137] a custom not entirely followed. On the coins, however, a symbol suggesting the Menorah was substituted — the cruse of oil that fed the lamps. It must nevertheless be emphasized that neither the amphorae nor the Menorah of Mattathias ever meant to suggest the Menorah or the oil of *Hanukkah*.[138]

In the collection of the Museum of the Jewish Theological Seminary there is a clay oil lamp of about the first centuries of the present era which can shed some light on the amphora of the large bronze coins of the Bar Kochba period. The lamp has six small openings for wicks, a large opening in the center for the oil, and a handle. In

[136] 40–37 C. E.

[137] R. H. 24a-b; Ab. Zarah 43a-b; Men. 28b.

The prohibition of reproducing the sacred objects, among them the seven-branched Menorah, was valid with regard to metals (as was the Menorah) and wood (as was the Menorah in the early days of the Maccabees). Menorahs, however, were made of other materials, such as stone and clay. One of them is the stone *Menorah* of Hammath-by-Tiberias. This prohibition was not carried out in early Jewish art (in synagogues and on tomb stones and clay oil lamps) where the seven-branched Menorah forms one of the main motifs. The reason may be that all of them have a background (frescoes, mosaics and relief) and are not independent as was the Temple Menorah. The *Menorah* on the coins and the intaglio of Mr. Newell belong to the above group. Concerning the prohibition of intaglios of rings-seals, to which the intaglio of Mr. Newell belongs, see the above first two talmudic sources.

[138] The story of the cruse of oil is very late (see p. 165). The designs on lamps mentioned in the following paragraph may explain the origin of this legend.

the space between the large opening and the small hollows is a structure of a temple with four diagonally fluted columns, pedestals, corinthian capitals, and with pediment and arch. In the middle, between the pillars, is an amphora with fluted body and scroll handles.

The building on the lamp suggests the Temple of Jerusalem. The amphora has almost the same form and fluted body as that on the large bronze coins of the Second Revolt.[139] The amphora on the clay-lamp appearing in the center of the Temple no doubt represents the vessel of oil which nourishes the flames in the lamp. The amphora on the large coins of the Second Revolt was then likewise used for oil for the *Menorah.*

Chapter X

Menorah

The Menorah appears on one of the coins of Antigonus Mattathias,[140] few varieties of the Menorah being known.[141]

The seven-branched Menorah was a compound of symbols: shape, parts, and lamp-direction. Its description is found in the Bible[142] and Josephus.[143] The semicircular shape of the *Menorah* on the coins is distinct, but its

[139] See note 110.

[140] Hill, XXIII, 11.

[141] Narkiss, III, 3.

The symbol on the obverse of the coin consisting of an object of a horizontal line from which rise four verticals, swelling in the middle and tapering to their tops, can be considered to represent either the four corners or horns of the golden altar or the four crowns (horns) of the Table of the Shew bread both of which were, like the Menorah itself, found in the sanctuary. This emblem may as well suggest the earth. As the Menorah symbolized the heavenly bodies (see below, note 27), the obv. may refer to the earth, believed then to be flat and supported by pillars (b. Hag. 12b).

[142] Ex. 25.31–40; 37.17–24.

[143] Ant. III, 6, 7.

details — the knobs, flowers, and cups are not shown.[144] Of importance, however, is the direction of the lamps, for this affords a better understanding of the Menorah itself and its symbols.

Post-biblical Jewish literature, from which reference can be drawn with regard to the description of the Temple, was recorded long after the destruction of the Temple. A discussion concerning the Menorah and its position within the Sanctuary reveals that knowledge of its correct orientation was not exact. Some scholars believed that the candelabrum stood in a south-northerly direction, while others maintained that it was in a east-western direction.[145] The problem also arose as to the direction of the seven lamps on top of the *Menorah:* whether the three lamps on either side faced the central lamp[146] or whether all seven lamps faced one direction, west.[147] The reason for the

[144] Perhaps due to the small size of the design on the coins.

Ginzberg holds that the knobs, flowers and cups are perhaps omitted in accordance with the Halaka not to reproduce exactly the furniture of the Temple.

[145] Shek. 24b; Men. 98a–b; *Braitha di Mlekhet ha Mishkan* (ed. Friedmann), X, 65, s. v. מערביים ומזרחיים.

[146] Sifre, Nu., *Behaalothha*, 59: נמצאו כולם מקבילים את האמצעי, they all (six) faced the central one. *Baraitha di Mlekhet ha Mishkan*, X, (ed. Friedmann, Wien, 1908), s. v. מערביים ומזרחיים היו דולקין כנגד נר האמצעי, שנאמר אל מול פני המנורה יאירו, מכאן היה ר׳ נתן אומר האמצעי הוא המכובד, the eastern and western lamps burned opposite the central lamp . . . Rabbi Nathan said, the central lamp one the honored one. See also Rashi to Nu. 8.2: אל מול נר האמצעי—אל מול פני האמצעי.

According to these passages the central lamp was called the Western Lamp which is against the possibility and reason if the Menorah stood in a west-east direction, an opinion held by the most of the Tannaim and subsequently decided by the Amoraim.

[147] Meg. 21b; Men. 98b: דתניא, אל מול פני המנורה יאירו, מלמד שמצדד פניהם כלפי נר מערבי, ונר מערבי כלפי שכינה, the priest entering the sanctuary to prepare the Menorah turned the fronts of the lamps toward the western lamp; and the western lamp toward the *Shekinah* (Holy of Holies). This was also the opinion of Maimonides. See his commentary to M. Tamid 3.9 and 6.1, s. v. מי שזכה: השבעה נרות איך היו—בין המערב ובין המזרח, ופיות כל הנרות לצד מערב, זה לאחור זה, כמו שהוא מצויר, והנר שאכתוב עליו א׳ הוא נר מערבי . . . ואל הסדר הזה נתכון באמרו אל מול פני המנורה

discussions was that the direction of the candelabrum and its lamps was based upon religious-cosmological conceptions, as they were symbols of the universe, and form of worship.[148] If the *Menorah* stood in a north-south direction, then the central shaft represented the sun, hence the three lamps on either side facing the sun suggested sun-worship a practice impossible in the 2nd Commonwealth. This combination eliminates the possiblity of a Western Light, for the lights facing the center, the sun, could not have at the same time also faced the West. The proper conclusion, supported by most rabbinic sources, was that the Menorah stood in a line parallel to the length of the Sanctuary, in a east-west direction, and the lamps faced the west.[149] The last lamps constituted the Western Light. Josephus, a priest during Temple times, states that the lamps had only one direction, a south-westerly, i. e. in a line running from north-east to south-west, with the lamps directed toward the south-west.[150]

This statement of Josephus is interesting. It establishes the fact that the Menorah stood in a direction running south-west, and the lamps upon it in the same direction

יאירו, רצה לומר שיהו פנויות כל הנרות לנוכח קדש הקדשים, שם פ"ו מ"א, ד"ה, החלו עולין במעלות האולם, the seven lamps were between east and west; and the opening of all lamps faced west, one behind the other, as it is drawn, and the first lamp (in the west) is the western . . . and this is the meaning of Nu. 8.2 . . . that all openings of the lamps shall face the Holy of Holies. The same opinion is held by *Ha Meiri*, to M. Tamid 3., p. 129: משנה זו על דעת האומר שמזרח ומערב היו הנרות עומדים, וכולם פיותיהם לצד קדשי הקדשים.

[148] See note 172.

[149] Tos. Men. 11.8; Men. 98a-b; Shek. 24b: כל הכלים שהיו במקדש, אורכן לארכו של בית, חוץ מן הארון, all objects in the sanctuary, their length paralleled the length of the House, excepting the Ark. See M. Tamid 3.10; 10.2: נכנס ומצא שתי נרות מערביים דולקים, מדשן את המזרחי ומניח את המערבי, the priest entered (the sanctuary) and found two western lights burning, he removed the ashes from the eastern lamp and left the western lamp burning. This reading in Tamid is the correct one, the others in the Talmud should be corrected according to this Mishna.

[150] Ant. III, 144 f.

but somewhat more to the south, in agreement with our thesis[151] that the West and the South-West were the Temple orientations. The Menorah symbolizing the planets,[152] would thus correspond to the accepted opinion in the time of the Second Commonwealth regarding the dwelling place of the Lord, that it was in the West, at a somewhat southern angle.[153] Because of the latitude of Palestine, the direction was set by the movements of the stars and planets of the western hemisphere which seems to have not a true west but a south-west direction, where they disappear beyond the horizon.[154] This direction was also that of the lamps of the Menorah, the end lamp at the west, near to the Holy of Holies. It was therefore called the Western Light or the Light of the Lord. This light had to burn without interruption, and was therefore called the Perpetual Light.[155]

In Mr. Newell's private collection there is an intaglio of the first century C. E., with a Menorah in the center and a cluster of grapes on the lower field of either side.[156] It is

[151] See chapter 2, p. 8, and p. 13, notes 53 and 55.

[152] Ant. III, 144 f.; Philo, Moses II, 102–103. y. Hag. 3.8 (89d): פעם אחת הטבילו את המנורה, אמרו צדוקים: ראו, פרושים מטבילין גלגל חמה, once the Menorah was immersed; whereupon the Sadducees exclaimed: look, the Pharisees are immersing the solar sphere; *Midrash Tadshe*, ch. 2: וכנגד המאורות נעשה המנורה; Nu. Rabbah 12.16: ברביעי — יהי מאורות ברקיע השמים, ובמשכן — ועשית מנורת זהב טהור, on the fourth day — let there be lights in the firmament of the heaven, and in the Tabernacle — and thou shalt make a candelabrum of pure gold (Ex. 25.31); Midrash Tadshe, ch. 11, Nu. Rabbah 15.5: These seven lights — corresponding to the seven stars (planets) that roam in the world: שבעה אלו שבעת הנרות, כנגד ז' כוכבים שמשוטטין בכל הארץ. See also b. R. H. 24a-b; Ab. Zar. 43a-b.

[153] See chapter 2.

[154] Neh. 9.6; See also preceding note.

[155] Ex. 27.20; Lev. 24.2–4; Sifre, Nu. 59.

[156] Resembling the fields of the coins of Rhodes. On some Rhodian coins Hellios-Apollo is shown crowned with ivy and grapes in the Dionysian manner. The intaglio of Mr. Newell may suggest a similar idea. The Menorah was the symbol of the solar system. See note 23.

significant that all lamps face one direction, as the Temple Menorah described above. The intaglio, once a setting of a ring, might have belonged to a priestly family.

CHAPTER XI

SECOND REVOLT — PROPAGANDA — COINS

More than sixty years had passed after the destruction of the Herodian Temple when the revolt of Bar Kochba occurred. The Jews still nourished the hope for political freedom and independence. The sign of the restoration of Palestine had been before Bar Kokba and in his time as well as centuries later the rebuilding of the Temple, which could signify the return of God's presence and grace.[157]

The Second Revolt against the Romans broke out. Bar

[157] M. R. H. 4.2: בראשונה היה הלולב ניטל במקדש שבעה ובמדינה יום אחד, משחרב בית המקדש התקין ריב"ז שיהא לולב ניטל במדינה שבעה, זכר למקדש, ושיהיה יום הנף כולו אסור. Formerly the *lulab* was shaken in the Temple during seven days and in the country only one day; when the Temple was destroyed, Rabbi Johanan ben Zakkai ordained that the lulab should be shaken in the country seven days, in remembrance of the Temple. He also ordained that during the whole of the day of the waving of the *Omer* the new corn should be forbidden. Ib. b. 30a: ושיהיה יום הנף כולו אסור, מ"ט, מהרה יבנה בית המקדש, וכו', that is the reason (for thr prohibition of the new corn on the day of the Omer), the Temple will speedily be rebuilt, and the Jews will say, 'Last year did we not eat the new corn from daybreak, now too let us eat.' See also b. Betza 5b. Cf. M. Ma'as. Sheni 5.2: כרם רבעי היה עולה לירושלים מהלך יום אחד לכל צד . . . שהיה רבי יוסי אומר משחרב בית המקדש היה התנאי הזה, ותנאי היה אימתי שיבנה בית המקדש יחזור הדבר לכמות שהיה.

Comp. also the daily prayer of *Rēzēh* in the *Amidah*. This was called to my attention by Prof. Ginzberg.

Cf. M. Ta'an. 4.8, end: וביום שמחת לבו, זה בנין בית המקדש שיבנה במהרה בימינו, אמן, and in the day of the gladness of his heart: that is the Temple, which will soon be built, Amen. See also Nu. Rabbah 15.7: וכשישוב הקב"ה ברחמיו ויבנה ביתו והיכלו.

Kokba found help and encouragement among leaders and scholars[158] and perhaps among many who belonged to or were related to the priestly class. The aim of the revolt was expressly represented in the types and symbols on the coins of that period. They were to familiarize the people with the ultimate goal of Bar Kokba and his followers — the restoration of the Temple and ritual, believed to be vital for the State and welfare of the land.[159] In this respect the Second Revolt coins could be characterized as propaganda coins — to stir the imagination and sentiment of the people in the war against Rome, to free Palestine and to reestablish the Temple by which the divine grace would be recovered.

The Bar Kokba period has thus produced coins — Temple series — of the Temple architecture and sacred objects, symbolizing the House of God and the ritual.

The main characteristics of the Temple architecture are best given by Josephus.[160] He describes the Tabernacle of Moses, but we may safely assume that his familiarity

[158] Y. Ta'an. 4.8 (68d): רבי עקיבא כד חמי בר כוכבה הוה אמר, דין הוא מלכא משיחה; *Echa Rabbati* 2.5, s. v. בלע ה'.

[159] B. B.B. 25b: ואמר רפרם בר פפא אמר רב חסדא, מיום שחרב בית המקדש לא הוגשמה רוח דרומית . . . ואמר רב רפרם בר פפא אמר רב חסדא, מיום שחרב בית המקדש אין הגשמים יורדין מאוצור טוב, since the destruction of the Temple, rain did not come from the south . . . since the destruction of the Temple, the rains are not from the good source. M. Sota 9.5, y. M. Sota 9.14 (23b): ר' שמעון בן גמליאל אומר העיד רבי יהושע, מיום שחרב בית המקדש אין יום שאין בו קללה ולא ירד הטל לברכה, וניטל פעם הפירות, רבי יוסי אומר, אף ניטל שומן הפירות, since the destruction of the Temple, there is no day without a curse, and dew of blessing did not descend, and the taste of fruit is gone . . . even the juice of the fruit. Cf. ib. 9.15 f. (24b).

Cf. b. Ber. 32b: ואמר ר' אלעזר, מיום שחרב בית המקדש נינעלו שערי תפלה, since the destruction of the Temple, the gates of prayer have been closed.

[160] Ant. III, 6, 4 (122 f.); ib., III, 7, 7 (181 f.).

with Herod's Temple helped him to describe that holy place which was erected more than a millenium earlier. The division of Herod's Temple corresponded in proportion to the division of the Tabernacle. It was divided into three squares, two given to the sanctuary and the third — to the Holy of Holies: "Internally, dividing its length into three portions, at a measured distance of ten cubits from the farther end (in the Herodian Temple the dimensions were double)[161] he set up *four pillars*,[162] constructed like the rest and resting upon similar sockets, but placed slightly apart. The area within these pillars was the sanctuary, the rest of the tabernacle was open to the priests. Now this partitioning of the tabernacle was withal an imitation of universal nature; for the third part of it, that *within the four pillars*, which was inaccessible to the priests, was like heaven devoted to God, while the twenty cubits' space, even as earth and sea are accessible to men, was in like manner assigned to the priests alone . . . The entire temple was called 'Holy (Place)', its inaccessible shrine *within the four pillars the 'Holy of Holies'*. . .[163] Furthermore there was made for God an ark . . . length of five spans, and a breadth and hight of three spans alike; both within and without it was all in gold . . .[164] To each of its longer sides were affixed *two golden rings*, penetrating the wood, and through these were passed gilt rods on either side,[165] by means of which it might, when necessary, be carried on the march . . ."

[161] M. Middot 4.7.

[162] Ex. 26.32: And thou shalt hang it upon four pillars . . . Ib. 36.36: And he made thereunto four pillars . . . See also Philo VI, *Moses* II, 80, 87.

[163] Ex. 26. 33.

[164] Ex. 25.10 f.; Jos., *Ant.* III, 6, 8 (134 f.).

[165] Ex. 25.12–16.

The Tetradrachm

The above is a description of the Temple motif on the tetradrachms.[166] The construction with the four pillars pictured on the coins represents the inner part of the Temple as described by Josephus. The dotted design between the columns suggests the Ark, hidden behind the veil.[167] The two circles in the Ark represent the rings or staves.[168] The oval lines above the Ark signifies the covering or the cherubs,[169] and the star over the Temple — divine glory.[170]

Characteristic is the fact that according to late Jewish

[166] Joseph C. Sloane Jr., Torah Shrine in Ashburnham Pentateuch, *JQR*, XXV, July, 1934, pp. 1–12, holds that the symbol on the tetradrachms represents a Torah shrine, and the circles of dots are door handles. However, the emblem on the tetradrachms is to be regarded as a temple, as the Ark motif is a later outgrowth of the temple motif itself. This can be borne out by the Dura frescoes where the Temple appears more than once. Moreover, there is no trace of doors on the coins.

[167] Ex. 26.33.

[168] Tos. Yoma 3.4–5: מזבח הזהב מבינתים כנגד שני בדי הארון . . . הגיע לשמאלו עם הפרכת עד שמגיע לארון, הגיע לארון ודחף את הפרכת במתניו ונתן את המחתה בין שני הבדים, the golden altar is in between, opposite the two staves of the ark . . . and he (the high priest) put the pan between the two staves. b. Shekalim 21b: ויאריכו הבדים . . . אלא נראין ולא נראין בולטין ויוצאין כשני דדי האשה, the staves were not seen, but protruded through the curtain and looked like two woman's breasts. Ib. y. 6.1 (49c); Cant. Rabbah 1.66: כך עד שלא נבנה ביהמ"ק היתה השכינה מתמצעת בין שני בדי הארון, משנבנה ביהמ"ק — ויאריכו הבדים, so until the Temple was built the *Shekinah* was confound between the two staves of the ark, but when the Temple was built, we are told, 'and the staves were prolonged' (I Ki. 8.8). Comp. Rashi to Cant. 1.13: he shall lie all night betwixt my breasts, — between the two staves of the ark.

[169] Ex. 25.19 f.; ib. 37.9.

[170] Rogers, p. 53; Madden, p. 239, suggest that the star is an allusion to Bar-Kokba. The name Bar Kokba has also been suggested to denote his birth place, *Kuziba*, in Judea (s. Klein, *Eretz Yehudah*, p. 162). Rogers, ib., holds that the wavy lines over the columns of some tetradrachms connote the pillar of fire, a theory difficult to accept, as the lines are horizontal. They rather suggest clouds representing divine presence. In the Bible God's presence is recognized by the appearance of clouds. See Romanoff, *op. cit.*, p. 74–77.

tradition the Holy of Holies in the time of the Second Commonwealth did not house the Ark of the Covenant.[171] It is quite possible that because of inaccessibility for the laymen to the sanctuary,[172] this fact was known only to the High priests and a few others, the general belief being that the Ark was there. The tetradrachms may suggest

[171] M. Shek. 6.1; ib. 21b f.; M. Yoma 5.4; ib. 52b; Tos. Yom ha Kipp. 3.6; *Braitha di Mleket ha Mishkan*, ch. 7; Cant. Rabbah 8.11.

According to R. Johanan (b. Yoma 14b), the Amora of the third cent., R. Simon of Mizpah was the author of the Mishna Yoma. See also Ginzberg, Tamid, the oldest treatise of the Mishna, p. 285 f. This would refer to the time of the Temple or soon after. It is the writer's assumption that the Mishna Yoma was written after the destruction of the Temple. The Mishna, 5.3, would suggest that there was an ark in the Temple of the Second Commonwealth. It reads: 'The outer curtain was held back by a clasp on the south side and the inner curtain on the north side. He (the High priest on the Day of Atonement) walked along between them . . . until he reach the ark. When he reached the ark he put the pan of burning coals between the two staves. He heaped up the incense upon the coals and the whole house became full of smoke . . .' However, this Mishna is immediately followed by Mishna 5.4 which is a direct continuation of the preceding one. It reads: 'After the ark had been taken away, there was a stone from the days of the earlier prophets, called the Shethiyah, three fingers above the ground, on which he would place (the pan of burning coals)'. . . The sense of the two Mishnahs is that their author wanted to describe the services, no doubt as a guide for the future, that theoretically (i. e., as it was in the Solomonian Temple), there was an ark, and the burning coals had to be put between the staves (note the omission of the mention of the cherubs), but since the time when the ark had been taken away, i. e. in the Second Temple, the High priest put the coals upon the rock that was there since the time of the early prophets — of Solomonian Temple. According to Jewish tradition originally the ark, as well as the Holy of Holies, stood above the rock. Cf. also Romanoff, *JQR*, 1937, p. 294.

Several traditions exist concerning the whereabouts of the ark. One is that it was hidden in the Wood Storage of the Temple, another that it was carried away to Babylon, a third that it was hidden in the Holy of Holies. Doubt existed as to whether there was a curtain in front of the Holy of Holies in the First Temple and whether or not there was an ark at all in the Second Temple. See b. Yoma 53b–54a; *Braitha di Mlekhet ha Mishkan*, ch. 7, s. v. והיכן היה הארון גנוז.

[172] M. Yoma 5.2, 3; M. Middot 4.5.

the rebuilding of the Temple, according to the Scriptures, with the Ark inside.

A great variety of coins with tetrastyle temples were struck in the second century.[173] In the center of the tetrastyle is represented a deity, or city-goddess. These coins explain the Jewish tetradrachms on which the Temple is pictured with four pillars. But in the latter case, instead of the deity there appears the Ark which may stand for the theophany.

---

[173] Hill, III, 1–2; VI, 10.14; XIV, 17–18; XVII, 3–4; and Aelia Capitolina coins, X, 4, 5, 7, 10.

SECTION FOUR

CHAPTER XII

GRAPES

THE grapes appear for the first time on the bronze coins of the First and Second Revolts in the form of a vine-leaf,[174] on the silver denarii and on some of the bronze coins of the Second Revolt in the form of clusters of grapes.[175]

The vine, grapes and wine[176] figure frequently in the Bible, as this produce constituted an important part of Jewish economics and in ritual. The cultivation of vineyards was one of the earliest forms of husbandry recorded in Scriptures,[177] and supplied the most important products with which the land was blessed.[178] It rated third among the choicest fruits of Palestine listed in Deuteronomy,[179] and this product was brought to the Temple as offerings of the first-fruits.[180] The vine was considered as represent-

174 Hill, XXX, 11–15; XXXVI, 6–9; XXXVII, 1–4, 7–11; XXXVIII, 1–2.

175 Hill, XXXVIII, 7, 14, 15; XXXIV, 1–3, 20; XXXV, 1–13; XXXVIII.

176 See I. Loew, Flora, I, 149–169.

177 Gen. 9.20.

178 Gen. 27.28; Ket. 111b.

179 Deut. 8.8. See note 180.

180 M. Bik. 1.3; 3.1, 3.

ing the trees.[181] In the Temple, wine was used as an offering upon the altar.[182] The vine and grapes decorated the sacred vessels in the sanctuary,[183] and a golden vine with clusters of grapes stood at its entrance.[184]

The vine and grapes had already in the time of the prophets become symbols of Israel.[185] In the Talmud, the vine is referred to as representing also the world, Jerusalem, the Torah, and the clusters — to represent the patriarchs, the Sanhedrin, and scholars.[186]

The vine and grapes have likewise in early times signified blessing and fertility. 'Israel will grow as the vine,' proclaimed Hosea.[187] 'Thy wife shall be as a fruitful vine,' are the words of the Psalmist.[188] Joseph, whose name has been associated with fertility,[189] and upon whose children

[181] IV Ezra 5.23 (ed. Charles): out of all the woods of the earth and of all the trees thereof thou hast chosen thee me — vine.

[182] Lev. 23.13; Nu. 15.5 f.; 28.14. Cf. also Jos., Ant. III, 9, 4; Wars V, 13.6.

[183] Jos., Ant. XII, 2, 9 (tendrils of the vine sending forth clusters of grapes, and bunches of grapes formed part of the decorations of the table for the shew-bread sent by Ptolemy to the Temple).

[184] M. Middot 3.8; y. M. 4.4 (41a); Tamid 29a; Hul. 90b: ונפן של זהב היתה עומדת על פתחו של היכל . . . כל מי שהוא מתנדב עלה או גרגיר או אשכול מביא ותולה בה; Jos., Ant. XV, 11, 3; ib. Wars, V, 5, 4. See also I. Loew, Flora, I, 182 f.

[185] Isa. 5.1 f.; ib. 65.8 f.; Jer. 2.21; 6.9; Ez. 19.10; Hos. 10.1; Hul. 92a; Esther Rabbah, ch. 9: נפן אמרה אני אתן את עצמי שבי נמשלו ישראל. Maimonides, to M. Middot 3.8, comments that the vine at the entrance to the sanctuary meant that the people shall be blessed as the vine, since it represents Israel. Cf. Cant. Rabbah 7.17: נשכימה לכרמים, אלו ישראל, let us get up early to the vineyard, this refers to Israel (Isa. 5.7); ib. 8.11: כרם היה לשלמה, אלו ישראל, Solomon had a vineyard, this refers to Israel.

[186] Hul. 92a. Also Ta'an. 7a.

[187] Hosea 14.8.

[188] Ps. 128.3. Exodus Rabbah 16.2: וכן האשה נקראת נפן, the woman is called the vine. Ber. 57a: הרואה גפן טעונה בחלום אין אשתו מפלת נפלים, he who sees in his dream a vine laden with clusters of grapes, his wife will not suffer from miscarriage.

[189] Gen. 49.22–26; Deut. 33.13–17.

the evil eye has no power,[190] is pictured as a vine growing beside a spring.[191] Wine[192] and oil were sprinkled before the bride and groom as a token of blessing.[193] The blessing over the wine and bread became the symbol of sanctification, in later Jewish ritual, *and was adopted as communion in Christianity.*

In Jewish art the vine and grapes figure on the mosaics and sculptures of the early synagogues, early burial places and tombstones, and on Jewish illuminated manuscripts.

The vine-leaf is found on the coins of the First Revolt; the vine-leaf and the cluster of grapes on the coins of the Second Revolt.

The symbols of the vine-leaf and of the cluster of grapes may be emblematic of the first-fruits, *Bikkurim.* Wine was presented not in liquid form but by clusters of grapes. These symbols may also suggest the *Sukkot* period which was also the vintage season.

CHAPTER XIII

THE LILY

The lily, *shoshanah,*[194] appears on the coins of Johanan Hyrcanus[195] and Alexander Jannaeus.[196] It was regarded as the choicest among the flowers. It graced the capitals

[190] Ber. 20a, 55b; B. M. 84a.

[191] *Onkelos* to Gen. 49.22: ברי דיתברך כגפן דנציב על עינא דמיא.

[192] Tos. Shab. 7(8).16–17: ממשיכין יין ושמן בצנורות לפני חתנים ולפני כלות, ולא מדרכי האמורי. מעשה ביהודה והלל בניו של ר"ג שנכנסו לכבול, והמשיכו אנשי העיר לפניהם בצנורות יין ושמן. This custom although practiced by non-Jews was not considered a foreign practice. Prof. Ginzberg considers it a practice taken over from the Gentiles.

[193] Ginzberg adds the custom of pouring wine over the circumcized child.

[194] The lily is to be considered a generic term. See Smith's *Dictionary of the Bible*, s. v. Lily; Augusta A. Temple, *Flowers and trees of Palestine.* London, 1929, p. 1f. See also I. Loew, Flora, II, 160–184, Lily; and ib., III, 193 f., Rose.

[195] Hill, XXI, 6–8.

[196] Hill, XXI, 11–13, 16.

of the two main pillars, Jachin and Boaz, which stood at the entrance to the sanctuary of the Temple.[197] The lily likewise decorated other objects of the holy place.[198] One of the most elaborate gates of the sacred enclosure which opened toward the east and the rising sun, was called the Eastern Gate. The top of this gate was beautified with a sculptured form which was called *Shushan ha Birah* — the castle Susa (Shushan).[199] It might have been so called

[197] I Ki. 7.19, 22; Jos., Ant. VIII, 3, 4.

[198] Jos., Ant. XII, 2, 9, the Table for the Shew-bread sent by Ptolemy to Jerusalem. See also the Letter of Aristeas (Charles, *Apocrypha and Pseudoepigrapha*, II, v. 68): the feet of the table had heads like lilies; v. 75: the mixing bowls — the brim was an ornament of lilies in bloom.

[199] M. Middot 1.3: שער המזרחי, עליו שושן הבירה צורה, the Eastern Gate, upon it was *Shushan ha Birah* form; and usually rendered by commentators: 'on which was portrayed the Palace or city of *Shushan* or Susa.'

Prof. Ginzberg holds that it cannot possibly mean an ornament of lilies for it would have then been rendered: *Shoshanah* or *Shoshanim*, and *Shushan ha Birah* seems as talmudic tradition would have it as referring to the City of Susa. The figure of the Persian kings were placed in some Babylonian synagogues (cf. R. H. 24b), and it is not at all far fetched that the Temple had a picture of *Shushan ha Birah* instead of a figure which was very objectionable to the Jews.

The above Mishna, Middot 1.3, is very interesting. It reads: "Five gates were in the *Har ha Bayyit*, the two *Huldah* Gates on the south served as entrances and exits, *Kiponus* (Gate) on the west as entrance and exit, *Taddi* (Gate) on the north did not serve any purpose, the Eastern Gate, upon it *Shushan ha Birah*, form, through which (sees) the high priest who burns the heifer and all her attendants go out to the *Har ha Mishḥah* (i. e. Mt. of Olives)." The expression עליו שושן הבירה צורה — upon it *Shushan ha Birah*, form,— seems to be an explanatory clause that was inserted in later tannaitic times. The second half of the last paragraph: "through which . . . *Har ha Mishḥah*," is found in M. Parah 3.6, and in a more perfect reading: "through it (or by it, meaning the *Kebesh* — ramp or bridge) a priest (not high-priest as in Middot, as the sacrifice was usually performed by a priest. For the expression 'high-priest' comp. Tos. Parah 2) who burns the heifer, and the heifer and all her attendants go out to the *Har ha Mishḥah*." There were buildings in the Temple which were called *Birah*. One of them was the *Beth ha Birah* (M. Zeb. 12.4: פרים הנשרפים . . . נשרפים בבית הבירה). The priest who was to sacrifice the red heifer was previously assigned to a chamber in the *Birah* that was in the north-east of the Temple area and which was called Stone House (M. Parah 3.1; b. Yoma 2a). This construction might have been identical with the

because of the ornament of lilies on it. Long after the destruction of the Temple, when traditions were forgotten, and explanations were sought to things unexplainable, political interpretations were given to this supposedly strange architectural feature. The Amora Hisda suggested the form of the *Shushan Birah* was to serve as a reminder that the Jews returned from Persia (Babylon). Yizhak b. Abdimi intimated that the *Shushan* was constructed by the Persian government to emphasize Jewish dependence and to insure loyalty of the Jews to that power.[200] Of the other sacred objects in the Temple, lilies adorned the rim of the brazen sea or laver[201] designed for the washing of the priests before they performed their divine duty.[202] This laver which stood south-west of the monumental steps that led to the sanctuary, and near the altar,[203] symbolized the pure water of which the heavens were supposed to be composed.[204] The sacred candelabrum within the sanctu-

Beth ha Birah or another one entirely. We also find that the entire Temple was called *Birah* (Yoma 2a; Zeb. 104b). The same reference to the Temple is found in the Bible (I Chr. 29.1, 19). According to the M. Kelim 17.9 (also b. Bek. 39b–40a; Men. 98a) וב' אמות היו בשושן הבירה, אחת על קרן מזרחית צפונית ואחת על קרן מזרחית דרומית, *Shushan ha Birah* was the name of a building, and *Shushan* would thus not mean the name of the Persian city but a descriptive name of that particular structure.

[200] B. Men. 98a; M. Kelim 17.9; Pes. 86a; Bek. 40a. Also Rashi to Men. 98a, Maimonides to Middot 1.3, and the other commentators follow the amoraic interpretation. If the amoraic explanation be accepted, then why should the Persian city have been represented on the Eastern Gate and not any other gate of the Temple? Babylon and Persia according to the geographic conception of those days was north of Palestine (cf. Git. 6a, B. B. 25b: והא בבל לצפונה דא"י קיימי').

[201] I Ki. 7.26. See also chapter V, Cup-*Omer*.

[202] Ex. 30.18–19; 40.30–32. Rashi, to Yoma 19a, regards the ten washings of the hands and feet of the High priest on the Day of Atonement as being from the same laver. For washing the hands and feet of the priests from Kiyyor (כיור), see also: M. Tamid 1.2; M. Zeb. 2.1; ib. 19b; 20a f.

[203] M. Middot 3.6; M. Yoma 3.6.

[204] Water, according to Jewish tradition, was created first, upon which the spirit of God moved (Gen. 1.2). The firmament consists of

ary, perhaps representing the solar system,[205] was adorned, according to the Bible, with flowers, and according to

water (ib. 1.6). Talmudic tradition holds that heaven was created first, since it consists of water (b. Hag. 12a; y. R. H. 2.5, 58a; ib. 2.1, 77a). 'Heaven'— *Shamayyim,* has been rendered into '*Sham Mayyim*' or '*Sa Mayyim,*' 'There is water' or 'Carrier of water' (b. Hag. 12a; Gen. R. 4.9). The genetic waters were divided into two parts, half of it forms heaven and half — the ocean, was believed in the early centuries of our era (Gen. R. 4.4). See also Yalkut Shim'oni, I Ki 7.185: עגול סביב, שהרקיע עגול.

[205] See chapter on the Menorah. Cf. also y. Hag. 3.8, 89d: פעם אחת הטבילו את המנורה. אמרו צדוקים: ראו, פרושים מטבילין גלגל חמה, once the Menorah was immersed; whereupon the Sadducees exclaimed: look, the Pharisees are immersing the solar globe (or sphere).

This Sadducean wit reminds us of the explanations given by Josephus and Philo about the Menorah.

The explanation of the symbolism of the Menorah should not be understood in the sense that in the Second Commonwealth sun-worship was in practice. Tannaitic and amoraic literature point to the contrary. The Mishna, Suk. 5.2, leaves no doubt concerning the averse Jewish attitude toward sun-worship, and the ceremony on *Sukkot* at *Beth ha Shoebah* and the proclamation: 'our forefathers who were in this place had their backs to the Sanctuary and their faces were directed toward East, and bowed East to the sun; but as for us, our eyes are directed to God (i. e. West)', demonstrated that. On the other hand, the same Mishna admits the former practice, during the First Temple, which Ezekiel (14.8) and other prophets witnessed. The Temple of Solomon was built in a direction running East-West, and faced East, the sun. The main gate was the Eastern Gate. The Second Temple was built on the same place and the same orientation. A change, however, occured in Jewish belief and ritual. Instead of the East, the West became the direction of importance. This was carried out without the necessity of changing the architecture of the Temple. The features of the altar and Sanctuary remained as before. The Holy of Holies or the western part of the Temple became the point to which the services in the Temple centered. The meaning of the sacred objects was likewise reinterpreted to agree with the new orientation. The Menorah was found in the First Temple in which solar practices are recorded. Josephus and Philo recognized that and thus presented the original meaning of the sacred objects.

In early amoraic times, and perhaps even earlier, the *Menorah* symbolized wisdom, because the oil that nourished the flames traditionally possessed that quality (M. Men. 9.5; ib. 85b. See also note 207). This explains the suggestion that he who wants to attain wisdom should in his prayer turn somewhat to the south because the *Menorah* stood on the southern side of the Sanctuary. (b. B. B. 24b).

later Jewish tradition these flowers were lilies.[206] The lily represented the world of flowers.[207] It symbolized human virtues such as righteousness,[208] purity and chastity.[209] One of these virtues has been befittingly illustrated by the character of the apocryphal work, "Book of Susanna" (Shoshanah).[210] In the words of the prophet Hosea, the lily became the flower symbol of Israel: 'I will be as the dew unto Israel, he shall blossom as the lily;' and the lily was also allegorically referred to in the Song of Songs,[211] and as a favorite simile later in Hebrew poetry.[212]

The lily, shoshanah, is used generically,[213] as it embraced other related flowers. Lilies had grown on hills[214] and in the field.[215] The choicest of lilies were those that grew in the valleys,[216] in the proximity of water. *Peraḥ* — flower in the Bible — is often rendered *shoshanah* — lily — in the Targum.[217] This flower was considered to be one

[206] *Targum Onkelos* to Ex. 25.31–34; Nu. 8.4, where *Peraḥ* is translated *Shoshanah*. See also Jos., Ant. III, 6,7 (144).

[207] IV Ezra 5.25: Out of all the flowers of the world thou hast chosen thee one lily. Cant. Rabbah 2.3: — . . . משל את הצדיקים במשובח שבמינים המשובח שבמינים כשושנה —, the righteous are compared by Scripture to the most excellent species (of plants), to the most excellent of plants — like the lily. In Paradise the righteous are to be seated in seven rows, and their faces will shine like the sun, the moon, sky, stars . . . lily (Lev. Rab. 30.2: ז' כתות של צדיקים . . . ופניהם דומות לחמה ולבנה, לרקיע, ולכוכבים, לברקים, לשושנה, ולמנורה הטהורה.

[208] Cant. Rabba 6.6. Also preceeding note.

[209] b. Sanh. 37a. The lily as symbol of purity was adopted in Christianity as the symbol of the Virgin Mary.

[210] Hosea 14.6.

[211] Cant. 2.1.

[212] ידיעות המכון לחקר השירה העברית, v. 2, p. 225: פיוטי ינאי; v. 3, p. 53: פיוטים ושירי תהלה מרב האיי גאון; v. 5, p. 144: משמרות דר' פנחס; ib., p. 77: ברכת חנוכה.

[213] The lily in Hebrew, as in Arabic, is generic. Besides the *Lilaceoe*, *Iridaceoe*, etc., it has been also considered to represent the lotus. See *Catholic Enc.*, XII, p. 154.

[214] Cant. Rabba 2.3.

[215] Cant. 2.16; 4.5; 6.2, 3; Matt. 6.28.

[216] Cant. 2.1; I am the rose of Sharon, and the lily of valleys.

[217] See note 206.

that bloomed rapidly, therefore it became a symbol of fertility.[218] It constituted one of the many kinds of spices used in ancient times.[219]

The musical instrument *shoshan* or *shushan* mentioned in the Psalms,[220] evidently had the shape of the lily, as is seen from the harps on the coins of the Second Revolt,[221] and also resembled the shape of the lily on the coins of Johann and Alexander Jannaeus.

Strange as it may seem, the lily on the Jewish coins resembles the Rhodus flower — the rose. This seeming inaccuracy is explained by the generic term of *shoshan* which might have included such flowers as the lotus[222] and even the rose.[223] In fact, the Midrash contains a few passages which speak of a soft lily,[224] and the excellent of this kind is the lily of the valley,[225] paralleling the rose of the valley. Besides these allusions, the Midrash specifically mentions a *shoshanah shel wered*[226] — a lily-rose — which grows in orchards, this species of lily-rose being the symbol of Israel.[227]

It is evident that when the lily was considered by the

[218] Cant. 7.3: thy belly is like a heap of wheat set about with lilies. This biblical passage, illustrated, is found on Jewish illuminated marriage contracts.

[219] Cant. 5.13.

[220] Ps. 45.1; 60.1; 69.1; 80.1.

[221] Hill XXXIII, 8 (three stringed); XXXIV, 11–14 (3 st.); XXXV, 1–4; XXXVI, 4–5 (four and six stringed). See Jos., Ant. VIII, 3.8.

[222] Charles, *The Apocrypha*, The History of Susanna, p. 647, note 2, assumes that Shoshan may be derived from Egyptian *šošn* — lotus. See, however, note 225 M. Shev. 7.6 where a flower לוטס is mentioned alongside with the ורד.

[223] See notes 245 and 246, and Rashi to Cant. 2.1.

[224] Cant. Rabba 7.7: סוגה בשושנים, אלו דברי תורה שהן רכין כשושנים.

[225] Ib. 2.3: אמר ר' אליעזר משל את הצדיקים במשובח שבמינים, ובמשובח שבאותו המין; המשובח שבמינים כשושנה, ובמשבח שבאותו המין — שושנת העמקים. M. Sheb. 7.6: הוורד והכפר והקטף והלוטס יש להם שביעית; ib. 7.7: ורד חדש שכבשו בשמן ישן, ילקט את הורד. הר"ש: וורד שושן. הר"ם: הוורד הם השושנים האדומים.

[226] Lev. Rabba, 23.3; Cant. Rabba 2.6.

[227] Cant. Rabba 2.6.

29808

Maccabean rulers as one of the symbols to be reproduced on coins, this aesthetic choice, emblematic of Israel, and known to others through the Rhodus flower, influenced the selection of this particular kind.[228]

Chapter XIV
Pomegranate

The pomegranate appears on the reverse of the Maccabean coins of Johanan Hyrcanus,[229] Judas Aristobulus,[230] Alexander Jannaeus,[231] and Antigonus Mattathias[232] between the double cornucopia;[233] and the reverse of the coins of Herod I;[234] and on the reverse of the *shekels* and *half-shekels* of the First Revolt.[235] On the latter the pomegranate may now be identified beyond doubt. The characteristic form of the symbol consisting of a bunch of three pomegranates on a single stem is recorded in the Mishnah.[236]

The pomegranate was one of the seven celebrated products of Palestine,[237] and among the first-fruits which were brought.[238] It won a place among the symbol-plants that

[228] The lily-rose may have had a solar meaning, as did the Rhodian rose, especially in view of its presence on the Temple objects. The red lily-rose resembled fire. According to Jewish cosmology, the sun consists of fire, and the throne of God is surrounded by fire.

[229] Hill, XX, 17–21; XXI, 1–5. Narkiss, *Coins of Palestine*, Part I, p. 97, identifies the lily as a pomegranate.

[230] Hill, XXI, 9–10.

[231] Hill, XXI, 15, 17–23.

[232] Hill, XXIII, 13.

[233] Charles, *The History of Susanna*, p. 657, note 2, holds that the 'poppy-head' is a lily.

[234] Hill, XXIV, 2–3 — full size fruits with the פיטום or top-piece.

[235] Hill, XXX, 1–9. Cf. Narkiss, על הסמלים שבמטבעות העבריים, Jerusalem, Lunz vol., Jerusalem, 1938, p. 199; L. Anson, *Numismatica Graeca*, III, *Agriculture*, XXX, 1408, considers them lilies; Madden, p. 67, *regards this emblem as Aaron's rod*; Hill, p. 269, stem with three flowers.

[236] M. Kelim 17.4: הרמונים שאמרו, שלשה אוחזין זה בזה.

[237] Deut. 8.8.

[238] M. Bikk. 1.3.

were employed in the Temple in Jerusalem. Two hundred pomegranates decorated each of the two columns, *Jachin* and *Boaz*, which stood at the entrace to the sanctuary.[239] Josephus, a priest in the last days of the Temple, narrates that pomegranates decorated the sacred candelabrum — the Menorah.[240] They formed an integral part of the sacred vestment of the High priest, as bells and pomegranates were suspended from his mantle.[241] They symbolized natural phoenomena. According to Josephus,[242] the bells suggested thunder and the pomegranates — lightning.[243] In this respect the pomegranate was symbolic of rain and of fertility. This may bear a relation to Rimmon, the god of thunder,[244] and perhaps to places in Palestine originally associated with that deity.[245] It is interesting to note that the pomegranate, together with other fruits, was selected as a decoration for the *Sukkah* in talmudic times.[246]

The pomegranate, whether because of its being an attribute or because of its refreshing juice and great number of seeds,[247] had early assumed the meaning of blessing and

[239] I Ki. 7.18–20, 42; Jer. 52.22–23; II Chr. 3.16; 4.16; Jos., Ant. VIII, 3, 4.

[240] Ant. III, 6, 7 (144). On the stone candlestick of Hammath-by-Tiberias are carved two kinds of plants. One of them resembles the pomegranate, the other — the lily. See Sukenik, *Ancient Synagogues in Palestine and Greece*, Plate XIIa.

[241] Ex. 39.24–26.

[242] Ant. III, 7, 7; Wars V, 5, 7; Philo VI, Moses II, p. 119: the pomegranate represents water and the bells, the earth.

Ginzberg considers the explanations of Josephus and Philo regarding the bells on the garments of the High priest as rather fantastic.

[243] Comp. Jer. 10.13: When he uttereth his voice, there is a multitude of waters in the heavens, and he causeth vapours to ascend from the ends of the earth; he maketh lightnings with rain, and bringeth forth the wind out of his treasuries.

[244] II Ki. 5.18.

[245] Josh. 19.7; Neh. 11.29: עין רמון, (cf. Josh. 18.17: עין שמש); Josh. 21.24: גת רמון; II Ki. 5.8: בית רמון.

[246] Sukkah 10a.

[247] *Zer'a*, זרע, implies both seeds and children. Cf. Lev. 22.4, 13; Isa. 7.13; 44.3; 65.23; II Ki. 11.1.

fertility.[248] It also connoted piety, good deeds,[249] and knowledge.[250] It is therefore natural that the pomegranate should become the symbol of Israel.[251]

In a warm climate like that of Palestine, the pomegranate served many purposes. Its juice formed a cooling and delicate drink,[252] and pomegranate gardens were plentiful in that land.[253] The central part of Palestine was known for the best pomegranates, especially Baden in Samaria.[254] The shell of the pomegranate and its crown were used as a dye,[255] and the shell of the pomegranate was also used in games.[256]

The form of the pomegranate as it appears on the shekels and half-shekels is usually in its budding stage, with a blossom (crown) on it.[257] On the other coins it appears

[248] The pomegranate as symbol of fertility is found on Jewish illuminated marriage contracts. In the collection of the Museum of the Jewish Theological Seminary is a *Ketubah* from Isle of Rhodes, 1830, upon which pomegranates are found. The character and designs of this Ketubah are oriental.

Ginzberg considers the pomegranate as a symbol of fertility only in European ornamental *Ketubahs*, and is not typically Jewish.

[249] B. Ber. 57a: רמונא פלגי, אם ת"ח הוא יצפה לתורה . . . ואם עם הארץ הוא יצפה למצות, וכו'. אפילו רקנים שבך מלאים מצות כרמון. Cf. also Erub. 19a; Meg. 6a; Hag. 27a; Sanh. 37a; Cant. Rabbah 4.3, 4, 6, 7; 6.11. In Paradise the righteous will enjoy the beauty of the pomegranate. See: אוצר מדרשים, פ"ד, גן עדן. Targum Sheni to Cant. 4.3: רומנא . . . דצדיקיא מתילן לקבלי, the righteous are compared to me (pomegranate).

[250] B. Ber. 57a; Cant. Rabbah 6.17; 7.17.

[251] Esther Rabbah 9: רמון אמר, אני אתן את עצמי, שבי נמשלו ישראל, שנ' כפלח הרמון רקתך, the pomegranate said: I am ready to serve that purpose, for Israel is compared to me.

[252] Cant. 8.2.

[253] Cant. 4.13.

[254] M. Kelim 17.5; Zeb. 72b; ib. 74a.

[255] M. Sheb. 7.3; M. Shab. 9.5.

[256] Y. Rosh Hash. 1.9 (57c): משחק בקליפי אגוזים ורמונים, one who plays with shells of nuts and pomegranates; M. Kelim, 17.15, Hullin 12b: הרמון האלון ואגוז שחקקום התינוקות למוד בהם את העפר או שתקנום לכף מזנים טמא, if children hollowed out a pomegranate, acorn, or nut wherewith to measure earth, or fashioned them into a pair of scales . . .

[257] Hill, XXX, 1–9.

in the stage of ripeness, round, with the *pitma* or top-piece.[258] Only on the coins of Herod I is the pomegranate large.[259] The form on the *shekels* and half-*shekels* is significant, for it corresponds to the biblical description in Canticles which speaks of the 'budding pomegranate,'[260] and the ripe pomegranate corresponds to the mishnaic expression 'pomegranate and its flower.'[261]

Along with the ears of corn and basket of fruit of Demeter, the poppy is likewise one of her attributes. The pomegranate and the poppy, both having numerous seeds, could be symbolically related. The small fruit which resembles a poppy appears on the Jewish coins between the cornucopiae.[262] This fruit which has been taken for a poppy is obviously a pomegranate, the circle representing the fruit itself and the horizontal line over it — the *pitma* or top-piece.

Chapter XV

Trumpets

On the denarii of the Second Revolt two trumpets are struck.[263] Of the many musical instruments in the Temple, the trumpets had their specific function. In the Bible we find that Moses was ordered to make among other sacred objects, two silver trumpets (*ḥaẓoẓerot*) for the Tabernacle.[264] These trumpets were used in the Temple after

[258] See notes 229–232.

[259] Hill, XXIV, 2–3.

[260] Cant. 6.11; 7.13.

[261] M. Sheb. 7.3; M. Orla 1.8; M. Ukzin 2.3; b. Ber. 36b; Hul. 118b.

[262] Comp. the shape of the pomegranate on the coins of Herod I with the pomegranates between the cornucopiae.

[263] Hill, XXXIV, 15.16; XXXV, 5–8.

[264] Nu. 10.2, 8; II Chr. 7.6. Jos., Ant. III, 12.6, gives a description of the trumpet that agrees with the shape of the coins: In length it was little less than a cubit, and composed of a narrow tube, somewhat thicker than a flute, but with so much breadth as was sufficient for admission of the breadth of a man's mouth. It ended in the form of a

the return from the Babylonian exile.[265] They were blown during the offering of sacrifices on weekdays, holidays,[266] and two trumpets were employed during the ceremony of water-libation on *Sukkot*, when two priests in solemn procession with trumpets in their hands marched from the *Azarah* (Upper court) down through the Women's Court to the Eastern Gate, blowing the trumpets.[267] Two trumpets were also used on days of fasting[268] when special prayers were proclaimed owing to the lack of rain.[269]

The trumpet was related to the *shofar* (horn) in many ways. The prophet speaks of the *shofar* and *ḥaẓoẓerah* as synonyms.[270] In the Temple on New Year two trumpets and *shofars* were blown,[271] and the same instruments were used during fast days for the purpose of invoking rain. In amoraic times the term trumpet was used for *shofar* and *shofar* for trumpet.[272]

The relationship of the trumpets to the blowing of the

bell, like common trumpets. See Sifrē, *Behaalothecha* (ed. Friedmann, p. 19): שתי חצוצרות, שיהיו שוות במראה ובקומה ובנוי, the two trumpets shall be alike in appearance, shape, and beauty. See also M. Tamid 7.3.

265 This passage in Numbers belongs to the Priestly Code.

266 Nu. 10.10. Cf. M. Tamid 7.3.

267 M. Suk. 5.2; ib. y. 5.5.

268 M. R. H. 3.3.

269 Most of the fast-days in Palestine were for rain. Cf. Ta'an. 11b–12b. The greater part of the tractate Ta'anit is devoted to fasts because of insufficiency of rain.

270 Hosea 5.8: תקעו שופר בגבעה, חצצרה ברמה, Blow the *Shofar* (horn) in Gibeah, and the *Hazozerah* (trumpet) in Ramah.

271 M. R. H. 3.3: שופר של ראש השנה של יעל . . . ושני חצוצרות מן הצדדין, שמצות היום בשופר . . . ובתענית בשל זכרים . . . ושתי חצוצרות באמצע . . . שמצות היום בחצוצרות.

272 Sab. 36a; Suk. 34a: אמר רב חסדא, הני תלת מילי אשתני שמייהו, מכי חרב בית המקדש, חלפתא ערבתא, ערבתא חלפתא . . . שיפורא חצוצרתא, חצוצרתא שיפורא, R. Hisda said: since the destruction of the Temple, the following three things have had their names interchanged. What was formerly called *ḥilpetha* is now called *'arabta* . . . and what was before called *shifora* (*shofar*) is now called *ḥaẓoẓertha*, and what formerly was *ḥaẓoẓertha* is now called *shifora*. See Ab. Zarah 47a. Cf. also M. Kinim 3.6: כיצד קולו (של איל) שבעה, ב' קרניו לשתי חצוצרות.

shofar on Rosh Hashanah when judgment is supposed to be passed on water,[273] the usage of two trumpets during water-libation,[274] and on days of prayers for rain, suggests their importance in the ritual. The trumpets on the denarii of Bar Kokba were a reminder of the former divine services and the blessing of fertility which was possible only with the reconstruction of the Temple.[275]

[273] On *Rosh Hashanah* the world was supposed to have been created (R. H. 8a, 10b, f.). The world according to Jewish tradition consisted originally of water. See R. H. 11a: תניא רבי אליעזר אומר מניין שבתשרי נברא העולם . . . ואותו הפרק זמן רביעה. See also Hag. 12a–b.

[274] Y. Suk. 5.6 (55a): Zeira said: the trumpets were blown only at water-libation.

From M. Tamid 7.3 we learn that trumpets were blown while the Tamid was sacrificed. It was different, however, at *Beth ha Shoebah*. Here the priests who blew the trumpets did not remain in the Inner Court or *Azarah*, but marched in procession through the Women's Court to the Eastern Gate blowing their trumpets. This was done only once a year, and on this particular night.

[275] See chapter XI: Second Revolt coins.

SECTION FIVE

CHAPTER XVI

STRING INSTRUMENTS AND WREATHS

Two kinds of string muscial instruments appear on the reverse of the coins of the Second Revolt.[275a] A lyre, *kithara*, of three strings is found on the silver denarii and bronze coins.[276] A lyre, chelys-shaped, with three strings is found on one denarius,[277] and chelys-shaped lyres of four, five and six strings with horns for arms, on the bronze coins.[278] The inscriptions on the reverse are: First year of the redemption of Israel; Second year of the redemption of Israel; To the deliverance of Jerusalem. The obverse has two kinds of emblems: a cluster of grapes,[279] and a wreath with a palm-branch in the center,[280] bearing the inscriptions: Simon, or Simon Nasi-Israel. It is interesting to note that the wreath with the palm-branch appears mostly on the coins with the lyre on the reverse. The

[275a] Hill, XXXIII, 8; XXXIV, 1, 11–14; XXXV, 1–4; XXXVI, 4–5; XXXVII, 5; XXXVIII, 3–5.

[276] XXXIV, 1, 11–14; XXXV, 1–4.

[277] Hill, XXXIII, 8.

[278] Hill, XXXVI, 4–5; XXXVIII, 5.

[279] XXXIII, 8; XXXIV, 1; XXXV, 1–4.

[280] Hill, XXXVI, 4–5; XXXVII, 5; XXXVIII, 3–5.

other instruments which we have already discussed are wind instruments, the two trumpets. The coins picturing trumpets have on the obverse an olive-wreath.[281] The same kind of wreath is found on the obverse of the lyres on the denarii,[282] while on the obverse of the bronze coins the wreath is in the form of a three-leaf laurel.[283]

Musical instruments were used in the Temple by the priests and Levites for jubilation and praise.[284] In Bible times praise — *Hallel* — was recited to the accompaniment of music, in which the *Nebel*, *Kinnor* and *Haẓoẓerah* these three instruments designed on the coins were prominent,[285] the lyre-*kithara* suggesting the *Nebel* and the lyre chelys-shaped the *Kinnor*. The olive and laurel wreaths used in celebration[286] are likewise depicted on these coins. In the center of the laurel-wreaths is a palm-branch.[287] This same palm-branch appears alone on the reverse of the denarii,[288] and on the obverse is a bunch of grapes or olive-

[281] Hill, XXXIII, 11; XXXIV, 15–16. XXXV, 5–8 have the cluster of grapes on the obverse.

[282] Hill, XXXIII, 5–6, 9–10, 12–13; XXXIV, 4–10, 17–19.

[283] Hill, XXXVI, 4–5; XXXVII, 5; XXXVIII, 3–5. The laurel-leaf appears also on the large bronze coins of the same period, XXXV, 14; XXXVI, 1–3, 10. The traditional number of leaves of the laurel is three.

[284] Num. 10.1 f.; Ezra 3.10; Neh. 12.27, 46; I Chr. 7.6; 25.1–7; II Chr. 5.13.

[285] II Sam. 6.5; I Chr. 13.8; 15.28; 16.42; II Chr. 5.12–13; 7.6; 8.14; Ezra 3.10–11; Neh. 12.27; Ps. 150; I Macc. 4.54.

[286] Wreaths were, it seems, worn by people during celebrations. See II Macc. 14.4: Alcimus presented Demetrius with olive-branches of the Temple. Cf. the olive wreath, y. Sota 9.16 (24c) and Lam. Rabbah 5.17. An olive-wreath was placed on the head of the ox when pilgrims with the first fruits marched to Jerusalem, M. Bikk. 3.3. In Mishnaic times in Palestine wreaths of ears (M. Ab. Zara 4.2) and rose garlands (y. Ab. Zara 4.2, 43d) were not used by Jews as these were employed on non-Jewish festivals. At present it is the practice in the Orient to decorate the *Sukkot* with wreaths of ears. See שנות חיים, Jerusalem, 1921, 27.5, p. 100.

[287] Hill, XXXVI, 4–5; XXXVII, 5; XXXVIII, 3–5.

[288] Hill, XXXIII, 7, 12–13; XXXIV, 2–3, 17–19.

wreath. The palm-branch, as has been pointed out,[289] had varied significance: it was used during the ceremony of water-supplication, during jubilation, and as a sign of grace and glory.[290] The palm-branch used for the water-ritual appears in two forms: as a bundle on the reverse of the tetradrachms, and as a single branch to the right of the ampulla on the denarii.[291] Praise or *Hallel* sung at Temple services and public celebrations was hailed by the carrying of palm-branches by the people.[292]

It is of interest to trace the custom of carrying branches in the Jewish ritual. In the Bacchus festival people carried ivy, and during the Syrian occupation of Judea the Jews were forced to do so.[293] In Palestine the custom of carrying palm-branches and other branches possibly developed from the *Sukkot* practice. The Feast of Tabernacles was an important holiday in the Jewish calendar. Great multitudes gathered in Jerusalem. Even pilgrims from Babylon and other neighboring lands of Palestine came to the Temple,[294] as that period was the most opportune time of the year for festivities, and important religious-national celebrations were set for that date. The dedication of the Temple and altar by Solomon,[295] the dedication

[289] See ch. Palm and Palm-branch.

[290] Cf. II Macc. 14, 3–4, Alcimus presented King Demetrius with a crown of gold and a palm. Cf. II Esdras 2, the pious are crowned and receive palms.

[291] Hill, XXXIII, 5–6, 9–10, 14–15; XXXIV, 4–6, 8–10, 20.

[292] M. Suk. 3.8. See also II Macc. 10.7, branches and fair boughs and palms were used during the rededication of the Temple by the Maccabees, and see I Macc. 13.51, when Simon recaptured Jerusalem and the Tower, he entered the latter with *Hallel*, playing musical instruments and bearing palm-branches. See also note 327.

[293] II Macc. 6.7. See also III Macc. 2.29, where it is told that the Jews were compelled to wear ivy-wreaths during the festival of Dionysus; and ivy-leaf emblems were forcibly branded on their bodies.

[294] M. Ḥallah 4, 10–11.

[295] I Kings 8.3, 65–66; II Chr. 5.3; 7.8 f.

of the altar after the return from the Babylonian Exile,[296] and the dedication of the walls of Jerusalem by Nehemiah[297] were set for the seventh month, *Sukkot* time. As this festival was associated with prayers for rain and considered the New Year for water, booths — *Sukkot* — made from branches of various trees were built.[298] Palm-branches were used in the ritual during the entire holiday, when *Hallel* was recited and music played. The custom of waving the palm or *Lulab* during the reading of *Hallel* is still preserved in Jewish ritual. The palm-branch thus became associated with *Hallel* and jubilation.

This custom explains the troublesome passages in II Maccabees[299] advising the celebration of *Hanukkah* as the Feast of Tabernacles. According to the author of this book the Temple was profaned by the Syrians and two years later cleansed by Judas on the 25th day of Kislev.[300] *Hanukkah* was associated with the discovery of the fire by Nehemiah, and that is why the author of II Maccabees emphasizes the miracle of the sacred fire at the dedication of the altar.[301] *Hanukkah* is actually the festival of the dedication of the altar — *Hanukkat ha-Mizbeaḥ*.[302] This dedication was fashioned after the celebration of the other dedications that were performed during *Sukkot*, especially in view of the fact that the Jews could not celebrate the *Sukkot* festival that year, as the Temple was occupied by the Syrians.[303] A new festival of dedication, in Kislev, the eight day period was adopted. During the *Sukkot* festival, which was also the time of dedication, the full

[296] Ezra 3.1–4. [297] Neh. 7.73; 8.14 f.
[298] See ch. 1, note 22.
[299] II Macc. 1.18 f.; 10.6–7.
[300] I Macc. 4.54; II Macc. 10.5.
[301] II Macc. 1.18 f.
[302] I Macc. 4.52 f.; Megillat Ta'anit 9. See also S. Zeitlin, Hanukkah, *JQR*, 1938, p. 1 f.
[303] II Macc. 10.6.

Hallel was sung[304] accompanied by the carrying of palm-branches,[305] and the usage of fair boughs for the tabernacles or booths.[306] At the Kislev-dedication, modeled after *Sukkot*, *Hallel* was also recited during a similar eight day period.[307] This explains the bearing of branches, fair boughs and palms during the offering of hymns of thanksgiving by Judas Maccabeus.[308] The recitation of the full *Hallel* is still practiced during the entire festival of *Sukkot* and *Hanukkah*.[309]

The symbols on the coins as observed at the beginning of the paper, have a homogeneous character, representing objects used in the Temple. The musical instruments on the coins may refer to the hope of Bar Kochba for the restoration of the Temple, which forms the main motif of the Temple theme on the tetradrachms, and are part of the group of symbols on the Bar Kochba coins taken from the *Sukkot* ritual. The clusters of grapes on the obverse of some of the coins suggest the date of *Sukkot*, which was also the vintage season.[310] We have shown that the trumpets were used on *Sukkot*, and we may conclude that the two kinds of string instruments were likewise used during this holiday. The Mishna relates that during the celebration of *Beth Hashoebah* on the night of the second day of *Sukkot*, four large candelabra illumined the Women's

[304] M. Suk. 4.1: ההלל והשמחה שמונה, The [recital of the whole] *Hallel* and the rejoicing [contined for] eight [days]; b. Sab. 21b: לשנה אחרת קבעום ועשאום ימים טובים בהלל והודאה, the following year [after the Maccabean victory] these [days of Hanukkah] were appointed a Festival with [the recitation of] *Hallel* and the rejoicing.

[305] Pes. 95b; 117a: אפשר ישראל שוחטין את פסחיהן ונוטלין את לולביהן ואין אומרים הלל, — is it possible that Israel sacrifice their Passover-offerings or take their palm-branches [on Sukkot] without reciting *Hallel*. See ch. Palm, note 13.

[306] See ch. III, Palm.

[307] See notes 31 and 36. Cf. Tos., Sukkah 3.

[308] II Macc. 10.7.

[309] Maimonides, Yad I, הלכות חנוכה, 3.5: דבכל יום ויום משמונת הימים אלו גומרין את ההלל; *Tur*, *Orah Hayyim*, 683: כל ח' ימי חנוכה גומרין את ההלל.

[310] See ch. V, Omer, note 108.

Court. Men of piety with torches in their hands danced, chanted and praised, while Levites played *Kinors*, *Nebels*,[311] *Meẓaltayim*, *Haẓoẓerot*, and numerous other musical instruments.[312]

As the traditional date for the Temple dedication was *Sukkot*, the symbols on the coins of the Second Revolt belong mainly to the *Sukkot* ritual. Moreover, these emblems offer an explanation why *Sukkot* is called "The Festival."

CHAPTER XVII

THE SYMBOLS AND INSCRIPTIONS

		Obverse	*Reverse*
(*Simon*)?			
½ shekel	AE	Two *lulabs* & citron שנת ארבע חצי	Palm-tree & two baskets לגאלת ציון.[313]
¼ shekel	AE	Two *lulabs* שנת ארבע רביע	*Ethrog* לגאלת ציון.[314]
⅓ shekel?	AE	*Lulab* & two *ethrogs* שנת ארבע	*Omer* (cup) לגאלת ציון.[315]
Johanan Hyrcanus			
	AE	Helmet ———	Double cornucopiae יהוחנן הכהן הגדל ראש החבר היהדים.[316]
	AE	Wreath יהוחנן הכהן הגדל [ראש ה] וחבר היהודים.	Double corn., poppy or pomegranate between them.[317]
	AE	Lily (*rose*) ——	Palm-branch יהוחנן הכהן הגדל וחבר היהדים.[318]

[311] The LXX translates it psalterion.

[312] M. Suk. 5.1–2.

[313] Hill, XX, 8. The inscriptions: obverse and reverse respectively: "Fourth year, half [shekel]"; "[Of the] Redemption of Zion." In the following notes the name Hill is omitted.

[314] XX, 9, 10. "Fourth year, quarter"; "Redemption of Zion."

[315] XX, 11–15. "Fourth year." Rev. the same.

[316] XX, 16. The horns parallel. "The high-priest Jehohanan head of the Jewish assembly."

[317] XX, 17–21; XXI, 1–5; XX, 17–19 'A' series, "The high-priest Jehohanan and the Jewish assembly"; XX, 20–XXI, 4, series without 'A'. XXI, 5, has the title "head" of the Jewish assembly.

[318] XXI, 6–8.

		Obverse	*Reverse*	
Judah Aristobulus				
	AE	Wreath יהודה הכהן הגדול וחבר היהודים.	Double cornuc., poppy or pomegranate between them.[319]	
Alexander Jannaeus				
	AE	Anchor ΒΑΣΙΛΕΩΣ ΑΛΕΞΑΝΔΡΟΥ	Lily (rose) יהונתן המלך.	320
	AE	Palm-branch יהונתן המלך.	Lily (rose) ———	321
	AE	Wreath יהונתן (ינתן) הכהן הגד(ו)ל וחבר היהדים (יהדים).	Double cornuc., poppy or pomegranate between them (with or without inscription: יהונתן המלך).	322
	AE	Anchor ΒΑΣΙΛΕΩΣ ΑΛΕΞΑΝΔΡΟΥ	Star of eight rays יהונתן המלך.	323
Antigonus Mattathias				
	AE	Double cornucopiae מתתיהו הכהן הגדל חבר היהודים.	Wreath ΒΑΣΙΛΕΩΣ ΑΝΤΙΓΟΝΟΥ	324
	AE	Cornucopia מתתיה הכהן (ה)גדל חבר יהדים.	Wreath ΒΑΣΙΛΕΩΣ ΑΝΤΙΓΟΝΟΥ.	325
	AE	Double cornuc., ear of barley between horns	Wreath מתתיה	326
	AE	Double cornuc., poppy or pomegranate	(Inscription blurred)[327]	
	AE	Horizontal with four vertical lines מת.	Menorah (seven branched) ΒΑΣΙΛΕΩΣ ΑΝΤΙΓΟΝΟΥ.	328

[319] XXI, 9–10.

[320] XXI, 11–12. "King Jehonathan."

[321] XXI, 13.

[322] XXI, 14–23. "High-priest Jonathan and the Jewish assembly"; "King Jehonathan." XXI, 17–20 with name Jonathan; XXI, 21–23 with name Jehonathan. For details of the Hebrew inscriptions, see Hill.

[323] XXII, 1–7; XXII, 8–12. "King Jehonathan."

[324] XXII, 13–18; XXIII, 1–4. XXIII, 2–4 with letters נא. On top of cornucopiae suggestion of fruits. "High-priest Mattathiah, Jewish assembly."

[325] XXIII, 5–10. Sometimes bunch of grapes hanging over.

[326] XXIII, 12. "Mattathiah."

[327] XXIII, 13.

[328] XXIII, 11. Obv.: horizontal line from which rise four verticals, swelling in the middle and tapering to their tops. Narkiss, p. 100,20, has two Hebrew letters, מת, an inverted abbreviation of Mattathiah.

		Obverse	Reverse
First Revolt			
Shekel	AR	Omer (cup) א, שב, שג, שד, שה, — שקל ישראל.	Three pomegranates [329]ירושלם הקדושה (קדשה)
½ shekel	AR	Omer (cup) א, שב, שג, שד, — חצי השקל.	Three pomegranates [330]ירושלם הקדושה (קדשה)
¼ shekel	AR	Three palm-branches רבע השקל.	Wreath [331]ד.
	AE	Amphora שנת שתים.	Vine-leaf [332]חר(ו)ת ציון
	AE	Amphora (with or without cover) שנת שלוש	Vine-leaf [333]חר(ו)ת ציון
	AE	Amphora (with angular handles) שנת שלש	Palm-branch ———.[334]
	AE	Omer (cup) שנת שלוש.	Palm-branch ———.[335]
Second Revolt — Tetradrachms			
	AR	Temple and Ark ירושלם	*Lulab & ethrog* [336]שנת אחת לגאלת ישראל

[329] XXX, 1, 3, 5, 7, 9. Years one, two, three, four, and five of the Revolt. Year one, etc., abbreviated. "Jewish shekel"; "Holy Jerusalem," first year. "The holy Jerusalem," the following years.

[330] XXX, 2, 4, 6, 8. Years one, two, three, and four of the Revolt. Years abbreviated as above. "Half shekel"; "Holy Jerusalem," "The Holy Jerusalem."

[331] XXX, 10. The palm branches tied together. Obv.: "Quarter shekel." Rev.: Within wreath, letter *Daled*, an abbreviation of (year) "four."

[332] XXX, 11, 13. Narrow-necked amphora, with fluted belly and small curved handles. "Year two"; "Deliverance of Zion."

[333] XXX, 12, 14, 15. Amphora as above, with conical fluted lid. "Year three."

[334] XXX, 16. Narrow-necked amphora with angular handles. Crude palm branch. Narkiss, p. 120,82, has the date in Hebrew: "Year three."

[335] Narkiss, p. 120,83. Cup, stem with knob, "Year three"; a plant resembling a palm branch. The coin is in a poor condition.

[336] Hill, XXXII, 1. Obv.: Building with four fluted columns; architrave shown by row of dots over continuous line; within, arched structure with two dots. Inscription: "Jerusalem." Rev.: Bound lulab, ethrog in left field. The way it is held during the service of blessing the lulab. Inscription: "First year of the redemption of Israel."

	Obverse		Reverse	
AR	Temple and Ark, star (cross) on top	ירושלם	*Lulab* & *ethrog*	שב לחר ישראל[337]
AR	Temple & Ark, star on top	שמעון	*Lulab* & *ethrog*	שב לחר ישראל[338]
AR	Temple & Ark, star	שמעון	*Lulab* & *ethrog*	לחרות ירושלם[339]
AR	Temple & Ark, wavy line on top	שמעון	*Lulab* & *ethrog*	לחרות ירושלם[340]
Second Revolt — Denarii				
AR	Grapes	שנת אחת לגאלת ישר[אל]	Palm-branch	שב לחר ישראל[341]
AR	Grapes	שנת אחת לגאלת ישר[אל]	Lyre (*chelys*)	שב לחר ישראל[342]
AR	Grapes	שמעון	Lyre (*kithara*)	שב לחר ישראל[343]
AR	Grapes	שמעון	Two trumpets	לחרות ירושלם[344]
AR	Grapes	שמעון	Lyre (*kithara*)	לחרות ירושלם[345]
AR	Grapes	שמעון	Palm-branch	לחרות ירושלם[346]
AR	Grapes	שמעון	Palm-branch	שב לחר ישראל[347]

[337] XXXII, 4–6. Obverse as above; over architrave small cross suggesting a star. At the base is a podium with vertical lines for pilasters. "Yerusalem." Rev. as the preceding. "Second year of the deliverance of Israel." The date, "second year," in the inscription is abbreviated. The same abbreviation of this year is found on the other coins of the Second Revolt.

[338] XXXII, 2–3. As preceding, with star over architrave. "Simeon"; "Second year of the deliverance of Israel."

[339] XXXII, 7–9; XXXIII, 1–2. As No. 26. "Simeon"; "Deliverance of Jerusalem."

[340] XXXIII, 3. Waved line over architrave. "Simeon"; "Deliverance of Jerusalem."

[341] XXXIII, 7. Hybrid, year one and two. "Year one of the redemption of Israel"; "Second year of the deliverance of Israel." Top of branch to left.

[342] XXXIII, 8. Hybrid. Inscription as in preceding. Lyre, *chelys*-shaped, with three strings.

[343] XXXIV, 1. "Simeon"; "Second year of the deliverance of Israel." *Kithara*-shaped lyre with three strings.

[344] XXXV, 5–8. "Simeon"; "Deliverance of Jerusalem." In Nos. 7–8, pellet between the trumpets.

[345] XXXV, 1–4. "Simeon"; "Deliverance of Jerusalem." *Kithara*-shaped lyre with three strings.

[346] XXXV, 9–10. "Simeon"; "Deliverance of Jerusalem." Top of palm branch to right.

[347] XXXIV, 2–3. "Simeon"; "Deliverance of Jerusalem." Top of branch to left.

	Obverse		*Reverse*	
AR	Grapes	שמעון	*Ampula* & palm-branch	שב לחר ישראל[348]
AR	Grapes	שמעון	*Ampula* & palm-branch	לחרות ירושלם[349]
AR	Grapes	שמעון	*Ampula*	לחרות ירושלם[350]
AR	Wreath	שמע	*Ampula* & palm-branch	אלעזר הכוהן[351]
AR	Wreath	שמע	*Ampula* & palm-branch	שב לחר ישראל[352]
AR	Wreath	שמעון	*Ampula* & palm-branch	לחרות ירושלם[353]
AR	Wreath	שמע, שמעון	Palm-branch	שב לחר ישראל[354]
AR	Wreath	שמעון	Palm-branch	לחרות ירושלם[355]
AR	Wreath	שמע	Two trumpets	שב לחר ישראל[356]
AR	Wreath	שמעון	Two trumpets	לחרות ירושלם[357]
AR	Wreath	שמעון	Lyre (*kithara*)	לחרות ירושלם[358]
Second Revolt — Bronze				
AE	Palm-tree	אלעזר הכהן	Grapes	שנת אחת לגאלת ישראל[359]
AE	Palm-tree		Vine-leaf	

[348] XXXIII, 14–15. One-handled *ampula* (jug) r., with fluted body; on r., palm branch. "Simeon"; "Second year of the deliverance of Israel." Note the spelling Israel, "Israel."

[349] XXXIV, 20. Symbols as on preceding. "Simeon"; "Deliverance of Jerusalem."

[350] XXXIV, 7, 10. Ampula without palm branch. Inscription as in preceding.

[351] XXXIII, 5–6. Hybrid. "Sim," abbreviation of Simeon; "Eleazar the priest."

[352] XXXIII, 9–10. "Sim"; "Second year of the deliverance of Israel."

[353] XXXIV, 4–6, 8–9. Note spelling of Simeon in Nos. 8–9; "Deliverance of Jerusalem."

[354] XXXIII, 12–13. On No. 12, "Sim," on 13, "Simeon"; "Second year of the deliverance of Israel." On No. 12, top of branch to left.

[355] XXXIV, 17–19. Top of branch to right.

[356] XXXIII, 11. Abbreviated form of Israel.

[357] XXXIV, 15–16.

[358] XXXIV, 11–14. *Lyre-kithara* with three strings.

[359] XXXV, 11–13. Hill claims that the palm-tree type is the reverse. The reader will note from the list of types-symbols that the obverse of the denarii and of the bronze coins of the Second Revolt consists of three motifs: Grapes, Wreath, and Palm-tree. In the present study, the Palm-tree is considered as the obverse. The same order is presented by Madden.

The palm-tree has two bunches of fruit. "Eleazar the priest"; "First year of the redemption of Israel."

	Obverse		*Reverse*	
		שמעון נשיא ישראל		[360]שנת אחת לגאלת ישראל
AE	Palm-tree	שמע	Vine-leaf	[361]שנת אחת לגאלת ישראל
AE	Palm-tree	ירושלם	Grapes	[362]שנת אחת לגאלת ישראל
AE	Palm-tree	אלעזר הכהן	Grapes	[363]שב לחר ישראל
AE	Palm-tree	אלעזר הכהן	Grapes	[364]לחרות ירושלם
AE	Palm-tree	ירושלם	Grapes	[365]שב לחר ישראל
AE	Palm-tree	ירושלם	Grapes	[366]לחרות ירושלם
AE	Palm-tree	שמעון	Grapes	[367]לחרות ירושלם
AE	Palm-tree	שמעון	Vine-leaf	[368]שב לחר ישראל
AE	Palm-tree	שמע, שמעון	Vine-leaf	[369]לחרות ירושלם
AE	Wreath	שמעון נשיא ישראל	Amphora	[370]שנת אחת לגאלת ישראל
AE	Wreath	ירושלם	Amphora	[371]שנת אחת לגאלת ישראל
AE	Wreath & palm-branch	.שמעון נשיא ישראל	Lyre (*chelys*)	[372].שנת אחת לגאלת ישראל
AE	Wreath & palm-branch	.שמעון	Amphora	[373].שב לחר ישראל
AE	Wreath & palm-branch	.לחרות ירושלם	Lyre (*kithara*)	[374]שמעון

[360] XXXVI, 6–8. "Simeon nasi Israel"; "First year, etc."

[361] XXXVI, 9. "Sim"; "First year, etc."

[362] Narkiss, p. 121, 86. "Jerusalem"; "First year of the redemption of Israel."

[363] Narkiss, p. 125, 103. "Eleazar the priest"; "Second year of the deliverance of Israel."

[364] Narkiss, p. 128, 111. "Eleazar the priest"; "Deliverance of Jerusalem."

[365] XXXVII, 6. "Jerusalem"; "Second year of the deliverance of Israel."

[366] XXXVIII, 10–11. "Jerusalem"; "Deliverance of Jerusalem."

[367] XXXVIII, 6–9. "Simeon"; "Deliverance of Jerusalem."

[368] XXXVII, 1–4. "Simeon," "Second year, etc."

[369] XXXVII, 7–11; XXXVIII, 1–2. "Sim," "Simeon"; "Deliverance of Jerusalem."

[370] XXXVI, 1–3. Large coins. Within wreath, "Simeon nasi Israel"; Amphora with fluted body, narrow neck, and curved handles, "First year of the redemption of Israel."

[371] XXXV, 14. Large coin. Symbols as on preceding. "Jerusalem"; "First year of the redemption of Israel."

[372] XXXVI, 4–5. Wreath with palm branch in center, "Simeon nasi Israel"; *Chelys*-shaped lyre, No. 4 with four strings, No. 5, with six strings, "First year of the deliverance of Israel."

[373] Narkiss, p. 124, 98. Large coin. "Simeon"; "Second year of the deliverance of Israel."

[374] XXXVIII, 3–5. Hybrid. *Lyre-kithara* with three strings. "Deliverance of Jerusalem" on the obverse, and "Simeon" on the reverse.

	Obverse		Reversi	
AE	Wreath & palm-branch	לחרות ירושלם.	Lyre (*chelys*)	שב לחר ישראל[375]
AE	Wreath	ירושלם	Amphora	שב לחר ישראל[376]
AE	Wreath	שמעון	Amphora	שב לחר ישראל[377]

Chapter XVIII

The list as presented above consists of sixty-five combinations of symbols on both obverse and reverse. The dies, as a closer examination of coins will show, are more numerous. The list affords an observation of the chronological introduction of the symbols, and a more definite conception of their groupings, as well as the mutual relationship between the symbols on either side of the coins.

"Simon." On the obverse the *lulab* and *ethrog* appear in pairs: two *lulabs* or two *ethrogs*. In two instances, on the quarter shekels, the *ethrog* (citron) alone forms the symbol on the reverse while the obverse shows two *lulabs*, thus the obverse and reverse together equal the group on the obverse on the half shekel consisting of two *lulabs* and *ethrog*. Inference of this may be found in passages in the Talmud[378] relating opinions of scholars of the second century C. E. as to the number of plant-species that make up the *lulab*, and the number of the *lulab* and *ethrog*. The appearance on the coins of symbols in pairs may be a reflection of an early ritual practice in which the *lulab* was employed. The talmudic passages would thus depict a later stage in the development and use of the *lulab*. If this

[375] XXXVII, 5. Hybrid. *Chelys*-shaped lyre. "Deliverance of Jerusalem" on obverse, and "Second year of the deliverance of Israel" on reverse.

[376] XXXVI, 10. Large coin. Symbols as on XXXV, 14–XXXVI, 1–3. See notes 58–59. "Jerusalem"; "Second year of the deliverance of Israel."

[377] Madden, p. 244, no. 39. Large coin. "Simeon"; "Seond year, etc."

[378] M. Suk. 3.4; ib. 31b.

was the case, then the coins of "Simon" would belong to an early period and before the time of the First Revolt. The *lulab* is a bundle of plants, from the center of which protrudes a palm-branch. The entire bundle is surrounded by small pellets — a suggestion of fruits, resembling the cornucopia appearing on the coins of Johanan Hyrcanus and on some of the coins of Alexander Jannaeus. This *lulab* differs in shape from the *lulab* on the tetradrachms of the Second Revolt. The place of the *ethrog* on the "Simon" coins differs from that on the tetradrachms. It is placed beside the stem of the *lulab* on the "Simon" coins, and on the tetradrachms it is placed higher, sometimes near the very top. On the "Simon" coins both the size and position of the *ethrog* form a part of the whole composition of the symbol while on the tetradrachms the *ethrog* does not form a composite part of the motif and is only loosely related to the *lulab*.

The *lulab* consist of four plant-species: palm, myrtle and willow bound together and *ethrog* (citron).[379] The one reciting the blessing holds the bundle in his right hand and the *ethrog* in his left. This law was already fixed in the second century as is evidenced by the place of the *ethrog* to the left of the bundle on the reverse of the tetradrachms. The problem of the individual species was not definitely set in the second century,[380] for R. Ismael held that three myrtles, two willow branches, one palm branch, and one *ethrog* make up the lulab. R. Akiba's opinion was that one kind of each species is sufficient. The former's opinion was later accepted and it became the practice for the future.[381]

The cup on the "Simon" coins has a short stem with

[379] Maimonides, Yad I, הלכות לולב, ch. 7, 5–6.

[380] M. Suk. 3.4.

[381] Maim., op. cit., ch. 7, 7. Tur, *Orah Hayyim*, 651. Maimonides holds that one may add myrtle branches to the bundle for the sake of beauty; also Tur, ib.

knob and narrow base. The container is larger in proportion to the stem. On the silver shekels and half shekels of the First Revolt, the cup has a better proportion, the stem forming half of the cup's height, and being more slender in form.

The above mentioned observations as well as the epigraphy are essential for the further study of the "Simon" coins.

Johanan Hyrcanus employed non-Jewish symbols and Judaized them by eliminating the non-Jewish types and preserving the symbols. These are the cornucopia and the lily-rose. The latter had already been used by the Jews as an ornament on other objects than coins. The palm-branch is here introduced for the first time.

Alexander Jannaeus introduced the star of eight rays. This symbol was found also on non-Jewish coins. The Greek inscription on the coins of Alexander Jannaeus appears only when the symbol is the anchor.

Antigonus Mattathias introduced the symbol of the Menorah and the object on the obverse of the coin.

During the First Revolt, the branch with the three budding pomegranates on the shekels and half shekels was introduced.[382a] This symbol remained the same throughout their coinage. The three palm branches tied together appear on the quarter shekel. The amphora and vine-leaf appear at this period for the first time on the Jewish coins.[383]

The symbols on the tetradrachms of the Second Revolt are the same in the entire series, although different dies were employed as is easily noticed by the spacing and form of the inscriptions and from the details of the symbols. On the obverse the changes consist mainly in the details above

[382a] The ripe pomegranate appears on some of the coins of Herod I.

[383] These two symbols, in various forms, are found on some of the coins of the Procurators.

the architrave, such as the star or wavy line, the diameter of the columns, and the podium on all excepting the coin of year one. On the reverse the difference is mainly in the size and position of the *ethrog*. On the coins of year one, the *ethrog* was evidently designed on the die after the inscription was completed, and the fruit was placed almost to the top of the *lulab* because of lack of space. The same thing happened perhaps with the dies of the other series, where one may notice that the inscription dictated the size of the *ethrog*. The feature of the *lulab* itself is interesting. It is a bundle of plants out of which three branches protrude. In the first century, as we see from the design, the most important features of the lulab were the palm branch, myrtle and willow, as here represented and defined.[384] The height of the palm branch corresponds to the minimum height prescribed later in the Mishna[385] to be not less than three hand-breadths, so that it could be shaken. The size of the *ethrog* on some of the coins agrees with the size given in the Mishna[386] that an *ethrog* small as a large nut might be used. The height of the three species is in accord with the rule found in the Talmud[387] that the palm branch should be at least a hand-breadth higher than the other two species, and likewise with the ties around the bundle.[388] The thickness of the bundle and the height of the *lulab* on the coins differ from the lulab found in Jewish art of the following centuries, and from the shape of the *lulab* in modern times.[389]

[384] M. Suk. 3.4. Concerning the form and amount of branches of the *lulab* in Gaonic times, see L. Ginzberg, *Geonica*, p. 309, 334; B. M. Lewin, *Otzar ha-Gaonim*, *Sukkah*, p. 41 f.

[385] M. Suk. 3.1. The proportional height was extended in amoraic times, the *lulab* to be at least four hand-breadths and the other species not less then three. Cf. Suk. 32b; Maimon., ib., 7.8.

[386] M. Suk. 3.5. [387] Suk. 32b. [388] M. Suk. 3.6; ib. 37a-b.

[389] In modern times the palm-branch is two or three times the height of the other species, and the entire bundle is thin.

The coins of the Second Revolt introduce the grapes on the obverse of the denarii and on the reverse of the bronze coins. The *ampula*, alone or with the palm branch to its right, is a new feature on the denarii of this period. The large fluted amphora on the large bronze coins now appear for the first time as do the musical instruments: the lyre in its varied forms and the trumpets. The wreath that appears on the coins of this time assumes special significance. The palm-tree on the obverse of the bronze coins has hanging bundles of dates. This tree first appears on a "Simon" coin with a basket on either side of the tree. It is also found on some of the coins of the Procurators, but on the coins of this period the palm-tree forms an outstanding motif.

Observing the list of inscriptions on the coins of the Second Revolt, one will notice that on the obverse the name of 'Simeon' appears most frequently. The other names on the obverse are: 'Eleazar the priest' and 'Jerusalem'. The title *Simeon Nasi Israel* appears only on the coins of the first year. On the reverse appear the dates of two successive years: 'First year of the deliverance of Israel'. 'Second year of the deliverance of Jerusalem', and 'Deliverance of Jerusalem.' Among the coins of the Second Revolt are four hybrids.[390] They belong to both years of the revolt.

[390] See notes 341, 352, 374 and 375.

INDEX TO PLATES

PLATE 1

Palm Tree

1 SIMON MACCABAEUS. Half Shekel, Year 4, Medium Bronze — Edward T. Newell Coll.
*B. M. C. pl. 20–8
See notes 4, 25, 29, 56, 58, 70, 73, 74, 78, 97, 313.

2 JUDAEA CAPTA, TITUS. Small Bronze — Louis S. Werner Coll.
B. M. C. pl. 31–3
Notes 4, 58, 63.

3 JUDAEA CAPTA, DOMITIAN. Medium Bronze — British Museum Coll.
B. M. C. pl. 31–7
Notes 4, 58, 63.

4 SECOND REVOLT. Small Bronze — Werner Coll.
B. M. C. pl. 38–6
Notes 4, 26, 58, 367.

5 SECOND REVOLT. Medium Bronze — Werner Coll.
B. M. C. pl. 37–8
Notes 4, 26, 58, 369.

6 SECOND REVOLT. Large Bronze — Werner Coll.
B. M. C. pl. Not Listed
Notes 4, 26, 58.

Palm Branch

7 JOHN HYRCANUS. Very Small Bronze — Werner Coll.
B. M. C. pl. 21–8
Notes 5, 32, 67, 68, 70, 289, 292.

8 HEROD 1. Medium Bronze — British Museum Coll.
B. M. C. pl. 23–14
Notes 5, 67, 68, 70, 289, 292.

9 FIRST REVOLT. Quarter Shekel, Year 4, Silver — British Museum Coll.
B. M. C. pl. 30–10
Notes 5, 25, 32, 67, 68, 70, 289, 292, 331, 383.

* = British Museum Catalogue, Greek Coins of Palestine by Hill.

10 First Revolt. Very Small Bronze — British Museum Coll.
B. M. C. pl. 30–16
Notes 5, 25, 32, 67, 68, 70, 289, 292, 334.

11 Second Revolt. Denarius — Werner Coll.
B. M. C. pl. 34–18
Notes 5, 32, 67, 68, 70, 288, 289, 292, 355.

12 Second Revolt. Denarius — Werner Coll.
B. M. C. pl. 34–4
Notes 5, 32, 67, 68, 70, 289, 291, 292, 353.

13 Second Revolt. Medium Bronze — Newell Coll.
B. M. C. pl. 36–5
Notes 5, 32, 67, 68, 70, 280, 287, 289, 292.

14 Herod Antipas. Medium Bronze — British Museum Coll.
B. M. C. pl. 25–6
Notes 5, 21, 32, 67, 68, 70, 289, 292.

PLATE 2

Lulab and Ethrog

15 Simon Maccabaeus. Half Shekel, Year 4, Medium Bronze — Newell Coll.
B. M. C. pl. 20–8
Notes 6, 25, 26, 29, 30, 56, 57, 66, 68, 70, 94, 97, 292, 313, 379.

16 Simon Maccabaeus. Quarter Shekel, Year 4, Medium Bronze — Newell Coll.
B. M. C. pl. 20–10
Notes 6, 25, 26, 30, 56, 57, 66, 68, 94, 97, 292, 314, 379.

17 Simon Maccabaeus. Small Bronze, Uncertain denomination — Newell Coll.
B. M. C. pl. 20–11
Notes 6, 25, 26, 29, 30, 56, 57, 66, 68, 94, 97, 292, 315, 379.

18 Second Revolt. Silver Shekel, Tetradrachm — Werner Coll.
B. M. C. pl. 33–3
Notes 6, 25, 26, 66, 68, 94, 157, 291, 292, 340, 379.

Ethrog

19 SIMON MACCABAEUS. Quarter Shekel, Year 4, Medium Bronze — Werner Coll.
B. M. C. pl. 20–9
Notes 7, 25, 56, 67, 68, 69, 97, 379.

Vine and Grapes

20 SECOND REVOLT. Denarius — Newell Coll.
B. M. C. pl. 34–3
Notes 8, 25, 32, 90, 175, 183, 185, 279, 310, 347.

21 SECOND REVOLT. Small Bronze — Werner Coll.
B. M. C. pl. 38–6
Notes 8, 25, 32, 90, 175, 183, 185, 310, 366.

22 HEROD ARCHELAUS. Small Bronze — British Museum Coll.
B. M. C. pl. 25–12
Note 22.

Vine and Grape Leaf

23 FIRST REVOLT. Year 2, Small Bronze — Werner Coll.
B. M. C. pl. 30–13
Notes 8, 25, 90, 174, 332, 383.

24 SECOND REVOLT. Medium Bronze — Werner Coll.
B. M. C. pl. 37–7
Notes 8, 25, 175, 369.

25 SECOND REVOLT. Large Bronze — Werner Coll.
Notes 8, 25, 174.
B. M. C. Not Listed

PLATE 3

Pomegranate

26 FIRST REVOLT. Silver Shekel, Year 3 — Werner Coll.
B. M. C. pl. 30–5
Notes 8, 25, 32, 35, 235, 248, 251, 257, 260, 329, 382.

27 FIRST REVOLT. Silver Half Shekel, Year 2 — Werner Coll.
B. M. C. pl. 30–4
Notes 8, 25, 32, 235, 248, 251, 257, 260, 330, 382.

Single and Buds

28 JOHN HYRCANUS. Small Bronze — Werner Coll.
B. M. C. pl. 20–21
Notes 8, 20, 25, 32, 35, 229, 248, 251, 258, 262, 317.

29 JUDAS ARISTOBULUS. Small Bronze — British Museum Coll.
B. M. C. pl. 21–9
Notes 229, 258, 262, 319.

30 ALEXANDER JANNAEUS. Small Bronze — British Museum Coll.
B. M. C. pl. 21-17
Notes 231, 258, 262, 322.

31 HEROD 1. Small Bronze — Werner Coll.
B. M. C. pl. 24–2
Notes 8, 20, 25, 32, 35, 248, 251, 259, 262, 382.

32 ANTIGONUS. Small Bronze — British Museum Coll.
B. M. C. pl. 23–13
Notes 8, 20, 25, 32, 35, 232, 248, 251, 258, 262.

Lily Rose

33 JOHN HYRCANUS. Small Bronze — British Museum Coll.
B. M. C. pl. 21–6
Notes 9, 25, 32, 194, 195, 206, 209, 227, 228, 318.

34 ALEXANDER JANNAEUS. Small Bronze — British Museum Coll.
B. M. C. pl. 21–11
Notes 9, 25, 32, 194, 196, 206, 207, 209, 227, 228, 320.

Cornucopiae

35 JOHN HYRCANUS. Small Bronze — British Museum Coll.
B. M. C. pl. 20–16
Notes 10, 12, 104, 316.

36 JOHN HYRCANUS. Small Bronze — Newell Coll.
B. M. C. pl. 20–21
Notes 10, 104, 317.

37 ANTIGONUS. Medium Bronze — Newell Coll.
B. M. C. pl. 22–14
Notes 10, 104, 324.

38 ANTIGONUS. Small Bronze — Newell Coll.
B. M. C. pl. 23–10
Notes 10, 104, 325.

PLATE 4

Laurel Wreath

39 JOHN HYRCANUS. Small Bronze — Newell Coll.
B. M. C. pl. 20–21
Notes 10, 286, 317.

40 SECOND REVOLT. Large Bronze — British Museum Coll.
B. M. C. pl. 35–14
Notes 10, 283, 286.

Wreath with Almonds

41 SECOND REVOLT. Denarius — Werner Coll.
B. M. C. pl. 33–13
Note 10.

42 SECOND REVOLT. Medium Bronze — Newell Coll.
B. M. C. pl. 38–5
Note 10.

Temple

43 SECOND REVOLT. Silver Shekel, Tetradrachm — Newell Coll.
B. M. C. pl. 32–1
Notes 27, 166, 167, 326.

44 SECOND REVOLT. Silver Shekel, Tetradrachm — British Museum Coll.
B. M. C. pl. 32–2
Notes 27, 166, 167, 168, 169, 170, 338.

45 SECOND REVOLT. Silver Shekel, Tetradrachm — British Museum Coll.
B. M. C. pl. 32–4
Notes 27, 166, 167, 168, 169, 170, 337.

46 SECOND REVOLT. Silver Shekel, Tetradrachm — Newell Coll.
B. M. C. pl. 32–6
Notes 27, 166, 167, 168, 169, 170.

47 SECOND REVOLT. Tetradrachm — British Museum Coll.
B. M. C. pl. 32–9
Notes 27, 166, 167, 168, 169, 170, 339.

48 SECOND REVOLT. Silver Shekel, Tetradrachm — Werner Coll.
B. M. C. pl. 33–3
Notes 27, 166, 167, 168, 169, 170, 340.

PLATE 5

Menorah

49 ANTIGONUS. Small Bronze — British Museum Coll.
B. M. C. pl. 23–11
Notes 143, 144, 328.

50 ANTIGONUS. Small Bronze — British Museum Coll.
B. M. C. pl. 23–11
Notes 11, 123, 135, 137, 140, 200, 328.

51 INTAGLIO. — Newell Coll.
Notes 137, 156.

52 Clay Oil Lamp. — Museum, Jewish Theological Seminary of America Coll.
Notes 138, 139.

PLATE 6

Star

53 Alexander Jannaeus. Small Bronze — British Museum Coll.
B. M. C. pl. 22–1
Notes 11, 166, 170, 323.

54 Alexander Jannaeus. Small Bronze — Werner Coll.
B. M. C. pl. 22–8
Notes 11, 166, 170, 323.

55 Second Revolt. Silver Shekel, Tetradrachm — Werner Coll.
B. M. C. pl. 32–4
Notes 11, 166, 170.

56 Second Revolt. Silver Shekel, Tetradrachm — British Museum Coll.
B. M. C. pl. 32–5
Notes 11, 166, 170.

57 Second Revolt. Silver Shekel, Tetradrachm — British Museum Coll.
B. M. C. pl. 32–8
Notes 11, 166, 170.

Amphora

58 First Revolt. Small Bronze, Year 2 — Werner Coll.
B. M. C. pl. 30–11
Notes 12, 25, 106, 108, 127, 132, 332, 383.

59 First Revolt. Small Bronze, Year 3 — British Museum Coll.
B. M. C. pl. 30–12
Notes 12, 25, 106, 108, 127, 129, 132, 333, 383.

60 First Revolt. Small Bronze, Year 3 — British Museum Coll.
B. M. C. pl. 32–16
Notes 12, 25, 106, 108, 127, 128, 132.

61 Second Revolt. Large Bronze — Werner Coll.
B. M. C. pl. 36–10
Notes 12, 27, 106, 110, 133, 139, 376.

Ampula

62 Second Revolt. Denarius — Werner Coll.
B. M. C. pl. 34–7
Notes 12, 27, 106, 109, 124, 125, 350.

PLATE 7

Omer Cup

63 SIMON MACCABAEUS. Small Bronze Shekel, Uncertain Denomination — Werner Coll.
B. M. C. pl. 20–11
Notes 12, 28, 56, 82, 97, 107.

64 FIRST REVOLT. Silver Shekel, Year 2 — Werner Coll.
B. M. C. pl. 30–3
Notes 12, 28, 82, 91, 98, 107, 329.

65 FIRST REVOLT. Silver Shekel, Year 3 — Werner Coll.
B. M. C. pl. 30–6
Notes 12, 28, 82, 91, 97, 98, 107, 330.

Trumpets

66 SECOND REVOLT. Denarius — Werner Coll.
B. M. C. pl. 34–15
Notes 13, 27, 263, 264, 268, 269, 271, 272, 275, 281, 284, 357.

Lyre

67 SECOND REVOLT. Denarius — British Museum Coll.
B. M. C. pl. 33–8
Notes 14, 27, 74, 221, 275a, 277, 279, 284, 285, 342.

68 SECOND REVOLT. Denarius — Werner Coll.
B. M. C. pl. 34–13
Notes 14, 27, 74, 221, 275a, 276, 284, 285, 358.

69 SECOND REVOLT. Medium Bronze — British Museum Coll.
B. M. C. pl. 36–4
Notes 14, 27, 74, 221, 275a, 284, 372.

70 SECOND REVOLT. Medium Bronze — Newell Coll.
B. M. C. pl. 36–5
Notes 14, 27, 74, 221, 275a, 278, 284, 285.

71 SECOND REVOLT. Small Bronze — British Museum Coll.
B. M. C. pl. 37–5
Notes 14, 27, 74, 221, 275a, 284, 285, 375, 390.

72 SECOND REVOLT. Small Bronze — Newell Coll.
B. M. C. pl. 38–3
Notes 14, 27, 74, 221, 275a, 278, 284, 285, 374, 390.

PLATE 1

PALM TREE

PALM BRANCH

PLATE 2

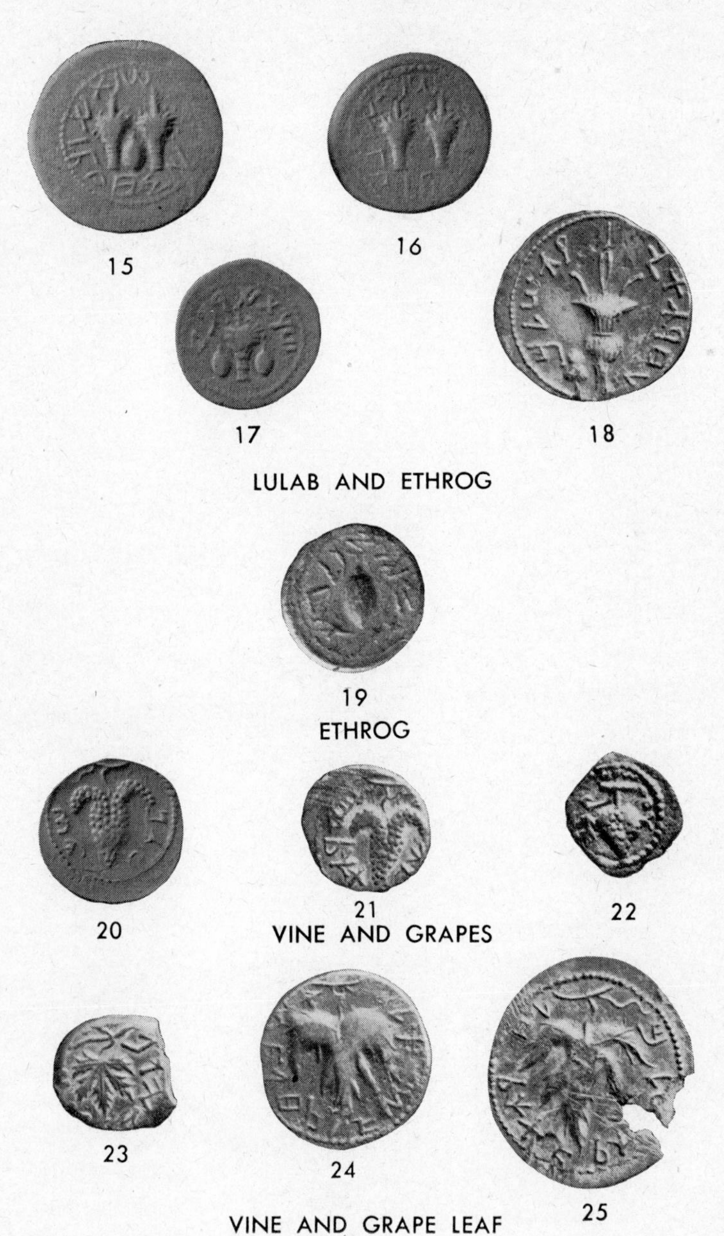

LULAB AND ETHROG

ETHROG

VINE AND GRAPES

VINE AND GRAPE LEAF

PLATE 3

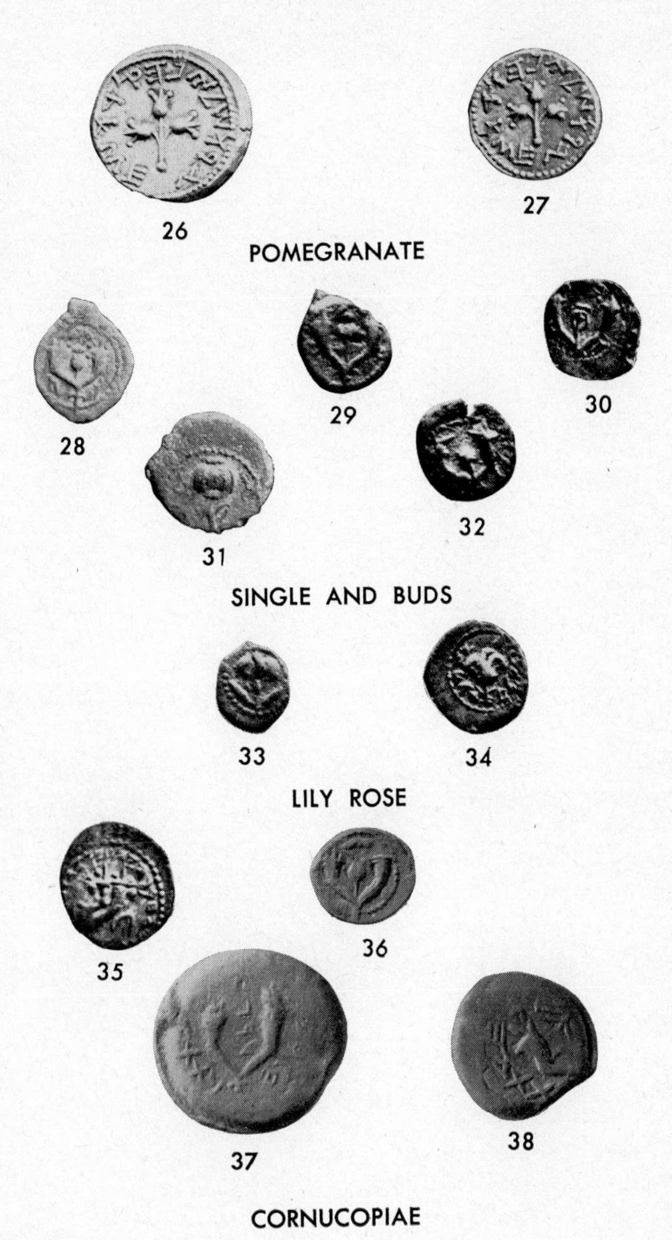
26
27
POMEGRANATE
28
29
30
31
32
SINGLE AND BUDS
33
34
LILY ROSE
35
36
37
38
CORNUCOPIAE

PLATE 4

39

40

LAUREL WREATH

41

42

WREATH WITH ALMONDS

43

44

45

46

47

48

TEMPLE

PLATE 5

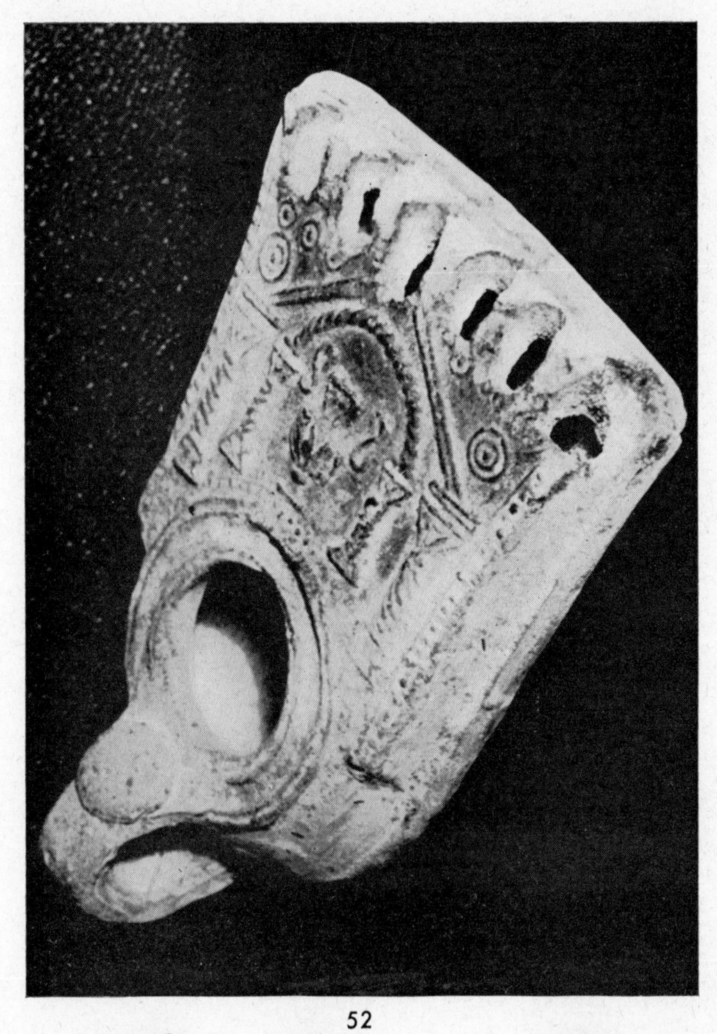

52

49

50

51

MENORAH

PLATE 6

PLATE 7

63 64 65

OMER CUP

66

TRUMPETS

67 68 69

70 71 72

LYRE